Into the M

Andrea Corrie

There is a saying in Tibetan,
'Tragedy should be utilised as a source of strength'.
No matter what sort of difficulties, how painful experience
is, if we lose hope, that's our real disaster.

Dalai Lama X1V

To Linda
Thank you for
being there
with love
Andrea xxx

Jan 2014.

ISBN 978-1905399-89-5

Cover Design by Duncan Bamford
http://www.insightillustration.co.uk

Author images
Page viii: Shaun Corrie
Back Cover: Alison Sheppey

PERFECT PUBLISHERS LTD

23 Maitland Avenue
Cambridge
CB4 1TA
England
http://www.perfectpublishers.co.uk

Dedication

This book is dedicated to both my children:
Stella Louise Gardener (nee Clark)
and
James Edward Clark
the wonderful and unique creations of my life.

Acknowledgements

*"We must find time to stop and thank the people who make
a difference in our lives. "*

John F. Kennedy

My book would be incomplete if I did not express my
thanks to those who help and support me in many ways:
Thank you to my family of course …Stella, my precious
daughter whom I love 'all the world', Sally, Janine, Mark,
Lizzie and Ben. Peter. David, Rosemary, Verity and
Michael.

I particularly wish to acknowledge the unstinting support
given to me by Pauline Grainger who is always there for
me. If I had a sister, she would be you, Pauline.

I am grateful to my longstanding friends, whether local or
far-flung – Sue and Greg, Lyndsay, Sylvi and Tim in
France, Stella and John in America and Karen in Australia
who are all just an email or a phone call away, and friends
and colleagues – Alison and Bob, George and Tony,
Madeleine, Jackie, Linda and Janet.

I am indebted to Dee who was tasked with being the first
person to read my early drafts; her pertinent comments
helped enormously with the edits.

It is a pleasure to acknowledge David Hampshire for
leading James' funeral service and providing us with
pastoral support through our family losses.

I am grateful to all those people whom I have connected with (either virtually or actually) through The Compassionate Friends and the Drowning Support Network, who have so ably helped and supported me from the start – and continue so to do. In particular, thank you to Nancy Rigg, the ladies who 'do lunch' (you know who you are!), Gay, Penny, Serena, Cris; and to Linda Sewell, Lin, Frances, Jan, Shaun, Kelly and Mitch, for sharing their writing freely in contributing to my book.

I am very appreciative that Stella, Ange and Jenna have permitted me to reprise their innermost thoughts in Chapter 6.

Thank you to all James' friends for knowing him, loving him, laughing with him, sharing his memories, and keeping on telling his story. Just some of the names from a long list are Amy, Emma, Lorraine, Sarah, Chris, Ange, Chloe, Adam, Caroline, Kellie, Corey, Jenni, Sally, Kat, Lucy, Kirsty and Gemma.

Thank you to those who came to live with us and who were already, or became, our friends and helped us regain joy in socialising: Lucy, Jules and Kyle, Rachel.

I am appreciative of those with whom I have connected through Reiki, and in particular my lovely teacher Celia (Seeliana) and June, as well as complementary therapy tutors Ina and Trevor. Through my most recent Reiki course I connected with my proofreader; I am grateful for your eagle eye, Ann.

Thank you to Tim and Gary at Kingston Council who proved to be such able and empathic facilitators for our riverside safety campaign. I am grateful too that the way was initially paved by Ann Sweeney, a colleague from so many years ago!

I am particularly indebted to the serendipitous meeting with my virtual friend (I am sure we will meet one day), the writer Jan Andersen, who has encouraged my writing ever since our first email exchange. Jan has kindly written the Foreword and led me to the excellent publishers of my book.

Finally, and most significantly, I must thank my dear, beloved husband Shaun who is, quite simply, the rock on whom I lean.

About the Author

Andrea Corrie has always read avidly and until now, would describe herself as a hobby level writer, never envisioning that her life circumstances would lead to the creation of 'Into the Mourning Light.'

She has a love of words that has proved valuable throughout her professional life as a medical secretary. Having worked for many years for Consultant Gynaecologists, she is now employed by a Consultant Gastroenterologist, enjoying both the PA role and the medical terminology.

In the 1990s, Andrea took an English Advanced Level course at night school for the pleasure of working with the written word. More recently, she has honed her skills by joining a local adult education course in creative writing. She also enjoys photography, particularly since the advent of the digital camera and has had illustrated 'how to' articles published online and in 'Surrey' and 'Women's Running' magazines.

She regularly goes out running; and at the other end of the leisure spectrum, Andrea practises Reiki, holistic massage and reflexology from home - when time permits.

Andrea lives in the UK with her husband Shaun and she enjoys spending time with him, her daughter and son-in-law as well as her stepchildren and granddaughter.

Disclaimer

All personal events contained within this book are true. However, some names have been changed or omitted to protect anonymity.

The author does not take responsibility for the opinions expressed by anyone else in this book, but is committed to protecting the privacy of those mentioned within the book.

The author does not take legal responsibility if anyone mentioned within the book voluntarily chooses to reveal their identity, or if any other individuals choose to reveal the identity of anyone mentioned herein to the media or otherwise. Indeed, if anyone recognises themselves from the actions described within this book, then that in itself is an admission of culpability.

In addition, any outside source, whether an individual or media source, takes full responsibility for the accuracy, timeliness and nature of anything said or published following the publication of this book. Neither the author of this book nor the publisher, take responsibility for anything said, claimed or published by a third party following the publication of this book.

Out of the Darkness

My tread was unsteady at dawn of fight
Held hostage to the terrors of the night
That seized me hard in dark embrace...tight
And black and full of fright
Then I longed to walk into the mourning light
And be content

But though I fought with all my might
To escape the rigours of this plight
I knew the future could just be bright
When grieving shadows cleared from sight
Then could I walk into the mourning light
And be content

Thus I flailed around me left and right
Swatting at tragedy's painful bite
Made up of pain and anguish and spite
Until the sombre clouds took flight
Surely I should walk into the mourning light
And be content.

My grief flies free, his spirit a sprite
That's rainbow hued like a silken kite
His shadow is ethereal and slight
And he lives in us from his heavenly height
Now I have walked into the mourning light
And I am content.

Andrea Corrie, October 2013

James in Brighton, October 2004

Foreword

by Jan Andersen
Author of Chasing Death: Losing a Child to Suicide

It came as no surprise to me when I learned that Andrea had included one of my favourite poems in her book, "Reason, Season, Lifetime". No-one crosses our path by accident; everyone we meet has a purpose, whether it is for us to teach a lesson, learn a lesson, to fulfil some sort of spiritual contract or to help each other in some way. Whatever the reason, and however painful the union, no contact is ever meaningless.

Andrea's path crossed mine as the result of the shared tragedy of losing a precious child and I feel privileged to know her. Although our sons passed over in different ways, there are many parallels within our grieving processes. My son Kristian and Andrea's son James both died as the result of a tragic set of circumstances. Therefore, in addition to dealing with the loss of our beloved sons, we are undoubtedly both plagued with the ongoing belief that their deaths were preventable. We also have to deal with the occasional lack of understanding from those who have never experienced such a tragedy themselves and therefore are ill-equipped to deal with our grief, which can manifest itself in inappropriate comments and platitudes.

As anyone who has lost a child will know, there is no "getting over it"; we simply learn to live alongside the grief. We are not living in the past when we talk about our children, but keeping their memory alive in the present. I think we have both learned that the only people who can come close to understanding our grief are those who have experienced child loss firsthand.

Andrea has shown immense fortitude in creating something positive as a result of what happened to James, at a time when many bereaved parents may struggle just to exist. In addition to initiating a campaign with Kingston Council to improve safety along the banks of the River Thames, Andrea has boldly chosen to be a voice for other bereaved parents in this book, not only to identify with survivors' pain, but also to educate others about the indescribable pain of child loss, in addition to honouring her son James. I am sure Andrea would claim that it is not bravery, but a catharsis and a desire to be a victor rather than a victim, but nevertheless all those who know her will view her as courageous.

The way in which Andrea articulates her innermost thoughts and feelings irresistibly draws the reader into her story and positions them right where she was at the time. I have no doubt that the eloquent way in which Andrea conveys the countless - and often unspoken - aspects of grief will resonate with many other bereaved parents. Despite the heartbreaking topic, the pace and flow of Andrea's writing is beautiful, enticing the reader to keep reading, with a measure of tears and laughter, on the journey from darkness into the "mourning" light.

"What moves through us is a silence, a quiet sadness, a longing for one more day, one more word, one more touch. We may not understand why you left this earth so soon, or why you left before we were ready to say goodbye, but little by little, we begin to remember not just that you died, but that you lived and that your life gave us memories too beautiful to forget."

Author Unknown

Contents

Introduction

What is the worst possible thing that can happen to a parent?

Surely, it is the loss of a child.

How do parents learn to live a meaningful, ultimately content life after such a traumatic event?

I hope to provide at least part of the answer in this, my personal testimony as mother to my much-loved nineteen-year-old son James, who died in an accident in 2005.

The purpose of my story is to share the undulating road of the grieving process and in doing so to provide encouragement to others who are suddenly bereaved; in particular those who have lost a teenager.

My story, which is also James' story, aims to help anyone affected by child loss within a family: parents, stepparents, grandparents, siblings, peers, friends, colleagues and neighbours.

I believe that it is also a useful tool to those training in counselling for supporting the bereaved as it highlights the emotions of grief and how they can be channelled successfully in a positive direction.
Bias has been avoided as far as possible but the basis of what I have written is necessarily my story, with contributions from others who share similar journeys.

It seems wrong to begin a book with death. The story thus starts with the birth of my son on 11 September 1985, which was the hottest day that year.

James Edward Clark, my second child, made a precipitous entry into the world, which seemed to set the pace at which he would live. I was in labour for a mere two hours and forty minutes. I remember that as the midwives wheeled me, in some haste, along the corridor to the delivery suite, I noticed in the corridor a couple of the small-wheeled cribs that the hospital used at the time. Each one contained a neatly folded pink blanket and I can recall saying, "We won't need a pink blanket for this one!"

I had been convinced that James was a boy since conception.

When he was born, I was euphoric, following the relative ease of his delivery, and although he arrived just after midnight, I could not sleep for the remainder of the night; I was high with the excitement and adrenalin of his natural birth.

But despite his rush to join us in the world, we soon found that James was not a particularly contented baby. He was sensitive to many allergens and throughout his younger childhood, he had periodic hospital admissions for acute asthma attacks. Perhaps surprisingly, this did not particularly perturb him but I am sure his spells in hospital contributed towards the empathy and sensitivity he showed towards other children. I remember one occasion very clearly. There was a very ill child in the opposite bed who could not communicate. James, who was only six or seven at the time, sat and stroked this boy's hand and read to him for long periods.

He was never a stereotypical macho or sporty boy; rather he was gentle and sensitive, which did not endear him universally to his peers.

He became known as the class clown at school. In an attempt to court popularity, he would be extremely silly and I was often called before the head of the school to listen to a list of James' misdemeanours. It was a pity because he was very bright, but he was totally non-competitive and he did not achieve the academic level that he could have. He always managed to do just enough work to get by.

Despite this, James was mainly a happy go lucky, caring character who looked up to his older sister (most of the time) and who, once he had escaped the disciplined confines of school, blossomed into a lovely student. The popularity that he longed for when he was younger became his as he matured.

I can't recall when James first voiced his desire to be a primary school teacher, but he applied himself to his studies sufficiently to get the grades he needed for a place at university in Brighton, Sussex. He loved his first year at uni. It was during the ensuing summer holiday that tragedy struck and James lost his life through drowning in the river Thames at Kingston, South West London.

In the first three years following his death, we campaigned successfully for safety improvements to be put in place at the riverside.

My book expresses my personal thoughts and beliefs, actions and reactions following my loss. However, it would not have been possible to write without the input from many others who have formed part of the whole process. If I am centre stage, there are those in supporting roles and some who hover quietly in the wings. I have done my best not to omit their contributions to the whole.

My innermost thoughts and emotions are laid bare in my story and I invite all those who walk the unbidden, unplanned and shocking path of bereavement to explore and share my journey through grief. Though the subject is poignant, my ultimate message is one of hope and positivity, and eventual recovery.

I believe that sharing the singularly personal experience of losing my beloved son will afford the reader greater insight to the wide-reaching effects of loss.

It takes strength and determination, and above all time, for each individual to find his or her way out of the pit of despair, along the road through the sorrowful darkness of grief and loss to come out the other side, as I have, into the mourning light.

Chapter 1

Ending and Beginning

*"When we least expect it, life sets us a challenge to test our
courage and willingness to change; at such a moment,
there is no point in pretending that nothing has happened
or in saying that we are not yet ready. The challenge will
not wait.
Life does not look back."*

Paulo Coelho

"Save me some cottage pie, please, mum"… perhaps it is
not surprising that my 19-year-old son James' final words
to me, apart from a cheery "See you later", were so
mundane. There was nothing to indicate that, after kissing
me goodbye and emphasising his exit with the usual slam
of the front door, on the evening of Wednesday 27 July
2005, he would not return. There was no inkling, no
presage of the trauma to follow, nothing to alert any of us
to the tragedy that was about to unfold.

Looking back, the day was so unremarkable in its
ordinariness that it seems impossible that anything
devastating could have occurred.

James was 19 and he was home for the summer from the
University of Brighton, where he had just completed the
first year of a primary school teaching degree. He was
enjoying the summer break, and despite my nagging,
showed little inclination to get part-time work, preferring to
spend vast amounts of time sleeping, pounding the PC
keyboard on MSN or catching up with his former college
friends. I was so pleased at the way he matured in his first
year as a uni student, and so glad to have his untidy, noisy

presence back at home, that I was being extremely lenient about his having to pay his way and - as ever - he had me wrapped around his little finger.

Just six weeks earlier, I had married Shaun, whom I met shortly after my divorce from Ken, the father of my children, in 1999.

At the time of the divorce, my daughter Stella was 16 and James 14. It was a very difficult period in all our lives but Stella and James showed great maturity and they managed to cope very well with the changes, establishing a comfortable rapport with their father until his sudden passing in 2002. By the time of our marriage, all our children - James, Stella, Mark and Janine (Shaun's two teenagers) - were very happy for us and with us on our wedding day. Shaun and I had taken our relationship slowly and this paid off in the acceptance of those around us of our tying the nuptial knot.

In retrospect, we are so glad we have our wedding day as a yardstick of happiness to which to aspire in the future. After the loss of a child, life can never be the same again, but I can attest that it is possible to enjoy life in a different way, which I call our new normality.

The devastation of a child's untimely passing is not something to be got over or recovered from. The best we can hope for is a reluctant acceptance and absorption of our inability to change what has happened, and to be able to pick up the pieces of our lives and move forward in as positive a way as possible.

I strongly believe that there are no shortcuts to the process of grieving, and it is an entirely individual road to travel.

There are no signposts and no indications as to the distances involved, in other words, no way of setting down the time it will take for each family member or friend to begin to come to terms with what has happened and be able to move forward in a semblance of normality.

If it were only possible to recapture a day that has passed; to recall with absolute accuracy and clarity, even a few hours of the day; to live it, breathe it, see, smell, hear and taste it, why then, I know exactly which day of my life with James I would choose.

That early July day in 2005, the weekend before his passing, was warm and sunny and James and I had decided to go out for a pub lunch together. We went out for one of what we called our 'heart to heart' lunches and he was on top form, telling me of his enjoyment of uni life and about his friends. He had impressed me with a real acceleration of maturity since he started uni. The only shadow was the fact that he had not worked hard enough in his first year and would need to repeat some modules, but we discussed this and I was confident that his attitude was very positive. I felt a swell of maternal pride as I watched my tall, handsome son stride up to the bar to order our lunch and drinks – it was one of the first times we had been out together on such a basis, now he was old enough to go to the bar to buy the drinks. It was quite a strange feeling, although James, being a typical hard up student had easily palmed a £20 note from me with which to pay for the lunch!

After lunch, we went for a walk.

"Look at that!" I exclaimed, as a brown 'comma' butterfly alighted on a leaf. "I never have my camera with me when I get a brilliant photo opportunity, typical!"

James put his arm round me, laughing, "Mum, I do love you. You're such an anorak with your photography."

We shared an easy affection and I felt on top of the world that day.

I often revisit that outing in my mind, and recall it with poignant pleasure. I especially remember James saying to me that he had never been so happy in his life and that he loved being 19. There is such bittersweet comfort in his words.

By mid-afternoon on Thursday 28 July, the first seeds of disquiet as to James' whereabouts had been sown in my and Shaun's minds. As a family, we were not unaccustomed to trauma. We had experienced a painful period of bereavement with the loss of my mother in 2001 and my father in 2003. Also, our house rules on keeping in touch had changed, in particular following the sudden death of Stella and James' father in 2002, and James became punctilious about always keeping in regular contact if he was away from home for any length of time, to minimise anxiety for all of us. When he had gone out the previous evening, he told us he might stay over with one of his friends, so we were not concerned during the following day, but when he failed to return home by 4.00pm, I sent him a text, just to enquire if all was well. I was surprised not to get a reply. (In hindsight, my anxiety was deflected somewhat by the fact that at the time I was suffering with a dental abscess, and unusually, I fell asleep when I came home from work).

I was awoken by the phone ringing at around 7.00pm. James' friend Amy, who had been among the group out with him the previous evening, was calling to ask if we knew where James was.

"We are worried because none of us has been able to get hold of James all day," she said.

My heart skipped a beat and I had a horrible feeling of sick worry in the pit of my stomach. I rang James' mobile immediately, and there was an automated message that indicated the phone was not working. We were now really concerned and fearful, and spent the remainder of the evening speculating as to his possible whereabouts.

Amy told us that the group had spent some time the previous evening in a nightclub "near the river at Kingston". As soon as she said this, my blood ran cold and I had a strong mental picture of my lovely son in cold, dark water.

I couldn't resist checking the location of the nightclub on the internet, and my imagination ran riot with varying scenarios of what could have befallen James.

Part of me already believed that he was in the river. Shaun did his best to reassure me not to think the worst and we eventually retired for the night with our anxiety levels running high, but at this stage, still hoping and believing that he would turn up safe and well.

Friday morning dawned, with no word from James. Anxious to keep things as normal as possible I set off to work, but my intuition did not allow me to settle, and by 11.00am we decided we must report James missing. Shaun contacted the police and I returned home to meet with a WPC and we gave her all the information that we could. She asked us many questions about our relationship with James, and his relationships with others, trying to build a picture and to establish if there was any discord, or any reason why he would not have returned home.

We found it very intrusive when she wanted to look in James' bedroom, and even study his diary for names and telephone numbers – anything, she said, which could provide some clues as to his whereabouts.

I can remember saying at the time that James would not be very happy to know a stranger had been poking about in his things. I had always respected his privacy and his room was his own space. It felt entirely wrong to be searching it even with valid reason.

Time dragged on leaden heels and we became increasingly anxious. Looking back, it is hard to remember how we passed the time; the constant questions ran through my mind like some kind of crazy litany: "Where are you? What's happened? Are you OK?"

We were acting out a parody of our normal life every minute of each hour – preparing meals we did not want to eat, watching television with little or no interest, and feeling heartsick. I was constantly alert for the telephone to ring or someone to approach the front door, all the time hoping it would be James breezing in as though nothing had happened. I jumped at the slightest noise and my heart pounded whenever I heard a car slowing along the road outside the house.

Apart from ringing the police for regular updates, there was little we could do once we had explored all the avenues of contacting James' friends, and pondering where he could be. The network amongst James' friends at that time was working hard to try to find him too. Social media was in its infancy at the time, but the entire group were able to send texts and make telephone calls.

I do not have the comfort of a formal religion but did I pray, did I bargain with God or the angels or whatever beings there are that watch over us? Yes, of course I did. I played a bargaining game in my head.

"If you send him home, if you make sure he has not come to any harm, I will never lose my temper/do anything wrong/I will become a saint…if it will only bring that boy home safe."

Saturday morning dawned; still no James. I stood in his empty bedroom with a sick feeling in my stomach. With every hour that passed without word from him, I felt increasingly convinced on some visceral level that something dreadful had befallen James and he was either injured or worse.

But hope remained. That morning I went to work again, partly to pass some time, and partly because my colleague was away, whilst in my heart something told me that I would not be in the office on Monday and I needed to set things straight.

I could not stop myself from ringing round various London hospitals to enquire whether they had had any emergency admissions, having wild thoughts that perhaps James was injured and had lost his memory. I drew blank after blank.

The sympathy I heard in the strangers' voices as I asked my futile questions almost undid me.

"Sorry," they said. "So sorry, but no, we don't have any young males who have forgotten who, or where, they are, today."

It was a crazy morning. I did not realise that the human mind could function on so many levels and that I could project a persona, which gave an impression to others that all was well, when in fact all was far from well. Perhaps the fact that I could type, check emails, make telephone calls, converse with the unfamiliar weekend staff in the corridors, all with a normal look on my face, was preparation for the mask that I would have to don in a short time.

I found myself unable to resist phoning Stella that morning. She had moved to Cornwall, the previous year when she was 21 and was happily settled in her new life there.

Although I did not want to alarm her, I felt she had to know that James was missing.

We exchanged platitudes, trying to convince ourselves that this was nothing out of the ordinary. But I know that Stella, like me, did not believe that any of the theories we explored such as James having amnesia or a lost mobile telephone, were in the least likely. We were used to living apart, but this was one of the times that the distance between us felt a great deal further than 250 miles. She offered to come home to Surrey but at that point, I persuaded her that it was not necessary.

Eventually (and almost reluctantly, for it was a safe haven of sorts), I left the office, satisfied that all the mundane tasks were up to date and my presence would not be essential first thing on Monday morning. There must have been some underlying process going on at a deep level of my psyche that told me things would change profoundly by the end of the weekend. I drove home.

We had another visit from the police, this time by a seemingly hard-bitten sergeant who took the view that perhaps James had "overdone the booze and stayed with his mates, you know, love, how lads do."

I found his attitude particularly patronising because I knew that James wasn't like that and that even if he'd had a lot to drink, he would have sent me a text to tell me his whereabouts. The sergeant plainly thought that James had gone to ground somewhere and I even took up his suggestion to send an email to James saying how worried we were and that he could come home – as if we had some minor disagreement. At this time, I remember asking the sergeant if the police could check the river but he disregarded the request as though it was ridiculous. The fact that James' mobile phone had ceased to work seemingly made no impression on the police either.

On Saturday afternoon, Amy came to the house. She and James met at college and were very close friends. Amy was distraught but through her tears, she kept saying to me, "Keep positive. We must keep positive."

But we looked deep into each other's eyes and I am sure that at that moment she felt, as I did, that the mercurial, quicksilver life force that was James had been extinguished. We just knew.

During Saturday night, there was heavy rain and I remember thinking at the time that if James was in the river, he would be found on Sunday because the water levels would alter. It was a morbid thought but it continued to nag at me throughout the wakefulness of the long night's vigil.

Sunday morning dawned, and no James. We rang the police requesting an update, and as had almost become routine by now, they said they would call us back.

I had a tremendous sense of foreboding. We did ridiculously normal things like shopping at the supermarket and cooking an egg and bacon breakfast that neither of us wanted.

I cannot imagine how we ate it, as we sat poring over the Sunday papers in our customary fashion, playing at being in denial of anything being out of the ordinary.

At mid-day, we saw a police car approaching our house. Shaun answered the door to two police officers, one of them being the hard-bitten sergeant, the other a pale young constable who looked little older than James.

I knew immediately by their set expressions that they had the worst news.

They came in and insisted that we sit down. My heart was pounding so loudly I thought that everyone must be able to hear it as the constable gave us the information, plainly and quickly, "A young man's body has been recovered from the Thames in Kingston this morning. He was seen in the water by various passers-by who informed the police. The ID that was found indicated it is most likely to be James".

It is almost impossible to describe the profound sense of shock that accompanied the news. I remember saying, "Oh no! Not my beautiful boy," over and over again to the young PC who told us. It was the first time he had reported a death to a family, and he was as white as we must have been. I found myself hugging him, and feeling unable to assimilate what I was being told. Incredibly and perhaps unbelievably, there was also a sense of relief that we now knew what had happened to James. The sergeant had the grace to look abashed that my worst fears had been accurate.

My head was instantly full of questions concurrent with the conviction that my heart already knew this was what had happened, days before.

The police had to question us as to whether it was possible that James would have taken his own life. I was emphatic on this point that there was absolutely no way, based on James' mental state on the evening he went out, that he would have considered this. He loved life, and embraced it with zest and pleasure.

How dreadful now to consider that all that life, all his vibrancy and his enthusiasm for his planned future, had been snuffed out by an unforeseen occurrence. I knew there was no way he would have done this to himself.

One of my concerns was that his death had been the result of violence at another's hand but there was no evidence to suggest that anyone else was involved in his demise. He had become separated from his friends, each small group of whom thought he was with the other. It appeared that he had simply lost his balance and fallen into the water. He had a fair amount of alcohol on board, and I later learned that in itself, this would have contributed to his inability to catch his breath when he fell into the water.

It is easy to conjure a mental picture of what happens when someone is unexpectedly immersed in water. Our views are coloured by myriad television images from fictional drama of someone struggling, crying for help, thrashing about in the water.

11

In reality, (although this is a generalisation), the shock of a fall and sudden immersion in cold water, especially when the faller's condition is already compromised by external factors, is sufficient to shut bodily systems down very quickly and irrevocably.

There is some comfort in knowing that James suffered for a very short time.

It is ironic that he was a strong swimmer.

As we tried to assimilate what we had been told, we quickly realised that the next task was to tell others what had happened. The most awful telephone call I have ever had to make in my life was to Stella.

It is impossible to imagine a worse conversation.
I have never wanted to hold someone as much as I wanted to hold my daughter at that moment, and to take away her pain. But of course, with two hundred miles between us, it was not possible. I had to hand the phone to the police sergeant to tell Stella what had happened.

I am sure it is not something that a police officer ever gets used to, but he was able to state the facts simply and unemotionally where I could not find the voice to do so. We were relieved she was not on her own when she received the awful news. Stella was with her boyfriend and a close girlfriend and I knew they would look after her until the following day when she would come up to be with us.

There were a number of people to whom we had voiced our concerns in the days of James 'missing' phase and they all had to be notified as well. I remember wanting overwhelmingly to have my mother near me, to hug me, support me and help me to assimilate this truly awful tragedy. Hot on that desire's heels, however, and in contradiction was a strong sense of relief that neither of my parents were here to be part of the shock and grief that already cast a pall over the house.

The rest of the day was taken up with telephone calls to spread the dreadful news and our shocked recital of the events became like a litany, as we answered the same questions from the horrified recipients of our calls.

There were so many people to tell, but on that first evening we contacted only our nearest and dearest because we were overcome with the shock and weariness that becomes a characteristic of early grief.

Shaun was amazing. He was truly a rock in his support of us all from the moment James went missing; something that only intensified when we knew what had befallen James. My love for my wonderful, gentle husband was unquestionably underlined day by day and continues to be so, with his calm support which is undeniably there for me in every move I make.

We held each other close after the police had left and tried to take in all that we had been told.

I will never forget his saying to me, "I wish I could take away your pain. If I could feel it for you, exactly as you feel it, I would."

The assurance of having his support at such a deep and loving level is beyond value and I try not to take it for granted.

With the news of James' death came shock, very real physical shock.

I can remember feeling that I wanted to lie down on the floor and become one with the earth, to sink into the ground and sleep forever, to avoid having to face this dreadful truth.

In fact, in the early days of loss, I often felt dizzy and slightly out of step with everyone else, as though everything was happening to me a millisecond after everyone else. Time passed strangely too, the days either being over in a blink or appearing to take an eternity. There was a constant sense of suspense, of waiting for something to happen in that terrible time of limbo between the death and the funeral.

Normal everyday things like eating seem too much effort and I had no appetite. We seemed to survive on tea and toast.

A level of denial, that I have seen described as reactionary disbelief, quickly took over almost as soon as we had James' death confirmed.

This is when the mind refuses to accept what has happened because it's all just too enormous and too terrible to take in. It is what gets you through the entire organisation necessary in the early days of loss. It is denial that makes you able to make all the telephone calls and calmly describe what has happened over and over again, almost like a recording. I can remember feeling so detached that I hardly considered the impact of my words on the recipients of the phone calls and their exclamations of shock or tears left me ostensibly unmoved.

It is a curious thing that when you are frozen with grief you can relate such awful news over and over without cracking and falling to pieces.

In the first few days, we were assigned two police family liaison officers and they became a valuable conduit in helping us to deal with the practicalities. We lived at the time in an area of Runnymede, which comes under Surrey police auspices, but James' accident happened in Kingston upon Thames, which is under Metropolitan police control. This meant that there was a need for communication between the two police forces whilst what had happened was investigated, and in fact we were very fortunate to have the support of these two officers whilst we wrestled with all the formalities. Any unexplained death in the UK requires investigation by the police and the attendant formalities such as a post mortem are obligatory.

There were some difficult questions to answer which were made easier by the gentle way our police liaison officers asked them.

We were not expected to formally identify James, something for which I was profoundly grateful, as I did not want to see him after he had been immersed in the river.

Instead, I was able to provide details of some distinctive marks that confirmed his identity beyond doubt. James and I share a familial abnormality of the little fingers that was passed down from my father, in that the first joint of the finger is displaced so that it faces inwards instead of parallel to the rest of the hand. Further, James had a birthmark on his foot, which also proved to be an identifying feature despite the fact I could not remember which foot had the birthmark.

I have never regretted not being able to see James after his death; for me it is far better to remember him as he was when he left to go out the evening of his accident. The coroner's officer with whom I spoke after James' post mortem was caring and I was able to feel that my son was being looking after with compassion.

The profound shock of such a sudden traumatic event somehow numbed me to such an extent that it allowed me to be able to sit in the funeral director's room and dispassionately discuss the wood we would like for James' casket, and gave me the strength that allowed me to deal with police, coroners and press with equal aplomb.

There was even an element of black humour – I am sorry if this appears distasteful, but we chose the Funeral Director largely on the basis that the representative was called Mr Ash, which I know is not in the least amusing, but it kept us going at the time.

Stella came to stay with us the day after James was found and I do not know how she coped with the journey to our home. I felt desperately sorry that she had to go through this latest loss and my feelings for her were mirrored by her feelings for me. We clung together a great deal both physically and emotionally. Shaun kept in contact with Mark and Janine and it must have been very difficult for them to take on board the fact that our new stepfamily had been so suddenly fragmented before it even had a chance to become a cohesive unit.

I found that I was able to deal with practicalities such as closing bank accounts, notifying schools/colleges etc, almost invariably dry-eyed. Denial is a blessed phase because I felt little or no pain, but it doesn't last. Reality keeps breaking through however much you try to ignore it.

I explore the process, the tenets and route of grieving more fully later on in my story.

The day after we lost James, I began to record my thoughts in a journal, finding that it helped me to express myself in the written word. The very first entry reads: "My pain is palpable. It has a life of its own that is kicking my heart and my stomach. Why did this happen to my beautiful boy?

I must go to Kingston to see where he spent his last moments.

Maybe tomorrow."

Comma butterfly on echinacea

Chapter 2

Find Me a Minister

In order to explain why we chose a Jewish Yorkshire man who lives in Cornwall to conduct James' funeral service, I have to look back to 2001, and my first, very painful experience of bereavement. My parents were Jewish; that is to say my father was brought up in London's East End in an Orthodox family. He met my mother, who was from Cardiff, during the Second World War, and they were a love match from day one. Mum studied under the auspices of the Chief Rabbi for two years to be accepted into the Jewish religion and, romantically, she and dad married secretly at a Register Office a whole year before she was allowed to stand up and be counted as a Jewish bride, when they had a further official ceremony – in effect, they were married twice. Although latterly they were not practising Jews, when mum fell ill and died over an eight-week period in 2001, dad wanted her to have a Jewish funeral, in accordance with her wishes.

My poor mum. Her illness, which turned out to be undetected Crohn's disease, galloped away at the most horrendous rate and despite various interventions and visits to the operating theatre, she passed away with my father, my brother and me at her side, in November 2001. In retrospect, the family felt we had missed signs that mum was unwell, but she was of the generation who say, "Oh, I wouldn't want to bother the doctor, dear" and also I know that being a person who valued her privacy, mum would not have felt comfortable discussing the intricacies of her digestive system with her GP.

Jews are somewhat thin on the ground in Cornwall, a county historically known as a Methodist stronghold. We explored various avenues but drew a disappointing blank. Our saviours were Ugalde and Son, the excellent Cornish funeral directors we employed. Somehow they managed to find a Jewish minister who at that time headed up a small Jewish community in Truro. It was arranged that he would come and visit dad to discuss the arrangements.

At this time Stella, James and I were all staying with dad until the funeral could take place. On the appointed day, we gathered expectantly, peeping surreptitiously through the kitchen window at the time of David's anticipated arrival. A sporty Peugeot screeched to a halt outside the house, the base thump of loud music emanating from its windows and out clambered a great bear of a man, sporting a long, greying beard.

"Wow!" said James, somewhat inappropriately, "It's Father Christmas!"

We were soon to learn that David possessed compassion, humour, reverence and an unstinting love of mankind in equal measures. He instantly took dad under his wing, and managed to elicit so many facts about mum from us all that he made her funeral service immensely personal, even though he had never met her. His warmth and affection made each person with whom he came into contact feel special. I remember dad being absolutely horrified after the funeral when David, having returned for the wake, quite cheerfully turned to and helped with the washing up.

Dad called me in a stage whisper and said in an appalled tone, "Stop the Rabbi, he's washing up!" But there was no stopping David; he was quite happy to muck in with the rest of us.

We kept in contact with David after mum's funeral, and he and his community remembered her in their prayers at significant dates in the Jewish calendar, which I know was a great consolation to dad.

Sadly, it was a mere 14 months before we had need of David's services again, and he was only too willing to take dad's funeral, giving an empathetic and sincere eulogy. Afterwards I recall he and James having a long discussion regarding the merits of Shakira versus Toni Braxton, and James finding it highly amusing that a man of the cloth could enjoy pop music!

I had, and still have, mixed feelings about my parents not being with us when James died. In the early days of loss, I longed to be enfolded in my mother's arms and have her make everything all right again, but it could not happen. Mum and dad would have been shocked and distressed at the loss of James, and at the same time I know they would have been very worried and anxious about how we would all cope, so in some ways it was as well they did not know of the death of their grandchild.

I like to think he has been reunited with them in spirit. In the dark days soon after James' death, I cried out in my mind to my mother, "My life is over. How can I carry on without my son?"

In reply, I heard her soothing voice, saying to me, "But darling, you can carry on. You will carry on. You have so much strength. You are stronger than you know and you will rebuild your life. It will take time, but you can do it."

My mother was an amazingly strong and resilient woman who throughout her life was in pain from arthritis, but she bore this with little complaint and much fortitude.

She was always a fantastic role model to me as a parent, as was my father, and I give a great deal of credit to my mum, in particular, for the wonderful relationship I have always enjoyed with my own children. Mum and I shared close confidences, and we seldom argued. Dad was more reserved but he was invariably supportive of my brother and me, whatever was happening in our lives.

We kept in sporadic touch with David, and in the fog of shock and grief that followed the news of James' death, I knew that he would be the ideal person to conduct the funeral service, if he was willing. The only problem was that I could not get hold of him for three days. I sent oblique texts, telephoned and poured out anguished emails to him to no avail. Finally, the phone rang and with relief I heard his lovely soft Yorkshire voice. He was actually on holiday with his sons in the North of England at the time, driving on the motorway. I asked him to pull into the next services, held on the line and then I just blurted out what had happened.

He immediately started to weep; he was simply distressed on our behalf. Over and over, he said, through his tears, "Oh no, what a tragedy, why that lovely boy?" interspersed with what I imagine were some fairly pithy Hebrew epithets.

Once I had told him what had happened, I had to ask him the important question – would he be prepared to conduct the funeral? I was immensely touched when he said, "Andrea, I would be honoured."

Despite being on holiday, David quickly made arrangements for his sons to stay with friends and he planned to come to us the following day and stay with us until after the funeral. It was a huge relief.

Having David to stay was certainly an experience, particularly when he stood in the garden in the morning to say his prayers, (Jewish praying is quite loud and dramatic).

David brought with him a wise and spiritual presence. The heavy atmosphere lifted with his wonderfully positive and kindly company. He somehow managed to raise our mood, through talking with us all individually, kicking a football round the garden with my nephew Ben, and helping with the preparation of food. He fitted in with whatever we needed even though we barely knew our needs.

In his own inimitable way, he brought God in through the door with him.

My emotions the day before the funeral were compounded by knowing that James was closer to us geographically than he had been since the day he went missing. The funeral directors had brought him back from Kingston to their chapel of rest in Addlestone. Ironically, this was next door to the pharmacy where James previously had a Saturday job.

I was amazed by the profound act of caring by James' former colleague in the shop, a lady named Sue who told us, on hearing that James died, that she had lost one of her best friends.

She knew he had been brought back to Addlestone and she took a pink rose into the funeral directors to be placed upon his coffin.

David was prepared to take a non-denominational service and it ended up being a fascinating hybrid of Judaism, Christianity and something in between.

23

I remember he took me to a quiet green space near our house and gave me a dress rehearsal of the words he planned to say on the day of the funeral, thus preparing me for the service and bringing an element of calm to my mind.

When we decided on the music, I asked James' friends for their choice of hymn. Without exception, they chose 'Shine, Jesus, Shine'. which apparently James was prone to launching into at the most inappropriate and random times. David gamely sang the words, but at the end of it he said, "James Edward Clark, only for you would I sing that!"

It was incredibly touching. We also played Aretha Franklin's 'Say a Little Prayer' and The Bangles' 'Eternal Flame'. James' taste in music was eclectic to say the least.

David's address was just perfect and I replicate it here. He said, "One of the things that defines us as human beings is that we are 'narrative beings'. By that, I mean we tell stories. We constantly tell our story to ourselves and to others – it is how we define ourselves. James had his own, unique, story and we remember that today. BUT more importantly, he formed part of our stories and therefore he forms part of the way we define ourselves. In that way, James will live on in us.

Of course, that story of James in our lives was different for each of us. To me James was the young man who mourned the loss of his grandparents. To his mother he was 'that beautiful little boy'.

To his family he was the 'grunting TV remote controller' of Sunday ensuring he'd caught up with that week's *East Enders*. To his friends he was what made a party a really good party: everything from singing as if he'd got a hot potato in his mouth to some of the strangest dance moves you were ever likely to see. To his tutors he was the boy who did just enough most of the time.

TO EVERYBODY HE WAS THE ONE WHO WAS THERE.

So, what characterised James? I suppose the easiest way to put it is: HE LOVED PEOPLE and as a result people loved him.

Whenever you were with James you were the most important person there, you felt special – he was everyone's friend. One way he achieved this was by keeping up contacts. So many of us have lost so many people over the years BUT James kept up the contacts; he made the effort, which didn't seem like an effort at all. BUT he didn't just keep friends – he made friends too. He was like the Sea of Galilee – the mighty Jordan runs into it and it teems with life, and it passes the Jordan where it runs to the Dead Sea, a sea that tries to capture the river and as a result cannot sustain life. James sustained life and he gave it to others. Part of that giving life was his inability to hold a grudge; James was an optimist and life was too short not to make the most of it.

There is an important concept in the Bible that a life cannot be judged by the number of years lived. Rather a life must be judged by the intensity with which it was lived. It is possible for a man to live 90 years and still not live half the life that James lived because he lived with such intensity. A man might have lived 90 years and be thought of as having a good innings; James did not just live 19 years, no, he had the best innings. Of course, that didn't mean that there weren't still things to do. Without a doubt he would have been an excellent teacher and a marvellous colleague;

25

he had dreams and those are sadly gone, BUT it was difficult to imagine James growing old, and being a teenager forever seems just right. Nevertheless, we can say – in the language of the Bible – James died full of days.

So our stories continue, all in some way shaped by James' story. I think it is important, though, that we don't define James solely by his death – that tragic boy who died in the Thames. On the contrary, we should define James by the way he lived and the way he altered all our stories for the better.

James will be missed. It is not fair that he died like this – so much perhaps left unsaid, but James will always be with us because he represented, for those who knew him, love and beauty – things that often seem missing from our lives. In the coming days let us continue to tell his story; at times it will make us laugh and at others cry – both are right. May he come to his resting place in peace."

When it comes to the awfulness of your child's funeral, you may feel like an observer, almost as though you are watching a film in which you are not the key player.

As the time for the funeral approached, there were moments when I felt so profoundly shocked by the reality of what was to happen that I did not think I would ever be able to breathe easily again. I felt a pressure within my chest that I can only describe as pure heartache. The passing of the hearse at the end of our road (I had expressly asked that we did not follow in procession to the crematorium) was a despairing moment.

I remember the truly dreadful weight of the silence when we arrived at the crematorium, the banks of mainly young people with stricken faces standing, many of them holding flowers and watching our arrival with dignity and stillness.

How strongly I wanted to remove myself from the proceedings. I rarely pray but I found myself saying over and over again, "Please God, give me the strength to get through this."

It has to be remembered that funerals are designed to allow tears. Whilst they are a celebration of a life, they are also underlining the ending of a life and the sadness of a young person's funeral cannot be over-stated.

How can you celebrate a life that has not been lived to a normal time span?

How, as a parent, can you bear to bury your child?

My memories of James' funeral are fragmented. They are small vignettes of the day that I do not care to visit too often. The true awfulness of the sight of the casket with its flowers on top is a searingly painful memory. We asked the attendees to wear bright colours – funereal shades were not for James and I was glad to see some colour around me. We numbered many; made up of family, friends, colleagues from James' part-time jobs, colleagues of Shaun and I – some of whom never met James - his teachers, tutors and many friends from the early days at nursery right through school and college to his year at university. Stella's friends came to support her too. We were almost overwhelmed by the love and empathy around us.

Stella found the courage to recite a reading for her brother. We chose a poem by Mary Frye written in 1932 (that coincidentally I had recently read in Sheila Hancock's memoir about John Thaw):

Do not stand at my grave and weep,
I am not there, I do not sleep.
I am a thousand winds that blow.
I am the diamond glint on snow.
I am the sunlight on ripened grain.
I am the gentle autumn rain.
When you wake in the morning hush,
I am the swift, uplifting rush
Of quiet birds in circling flight.
I am the soft starlight at night.
Do not stand at my grave and weep.
I am not there, I do not sleep.
Do not stand at my grave and cry.
I am not there, I did not die!

The words seem particularly poignant for a young person's death.

After the funeral service, I do not know how I kept my composure as one after one, the people who knew James filed past us and shared a few words. I met many young people who had known James from college and university; young people who had travelled considerable distances to pay their respects. Over and over again, I heard, "We loved James; he was just the best friend."

The love and compassion coming from all these youngsters was tangible and moving. I remember in particular one couple who stood out because they were dressed as Goths, complete with startling hair and makeup. Their faces were totally white and I am not sure whether this was from makeup or emotion. They had stood steadfast and dry-eyed holding hands throughout the service and they approached me, saying, "We are so grateful to James because he introduced us at a party two years ago, and we have been a couple ever since."

I began to realise that James had inhabited a world that I knew nothing about and it was both uplifting and comforting.

Inevitably, there were people who wanted to attend James' funeral but were unable to get there for one reason or another. One such was Sylvi, who lives in France. She and I have been close friends for almost 30 years and our children spent a great deal of happy times together during their childhood.

As the time of the service approached, Sylvi went to the local chapel in the village of St Germain de Confolens and sat with us in spirit throughout. Afterwards she sent me some photos from the chapel and described how the sunlight was streaming through the windows, making the dust motes dance in the still air. I was very touched that she involved herself in paying her respects to us all at a distance.

I had a telephone call from my friend Stella in the USA who also observed the time of the service, despite the time difference.

I felt uplifted by the knowledge that people were thinking of us at such a truly difficult time. Among the condolence cards and flowers that filled our lounge, there was unexpected kindness from people I have never met.
As part of my interest in photography, I belonged to a small, friendly photo critique group, 'Through the Lens',

whose members share their images online; a helpful aid to increasing photographic skills. The members are widespread in Australia, the USA and Canada. The group is ably headed up by my South African 'virtual' friend Hal, who lives in Australia. He and I began exchanging emails regarding photography - and life in general - as long as a decade ago.

On the day of James' funeral the florist delivered a bouquet, sent from all the members of 'Through the Lens.' Hal had coordinated this generous gesture, which I found very touching

Eventually we returned home and spent some time outside in the garden with those who followed us back for the post funeral wake. There was plenty to eat and drink, courtesy of the kindness of our neighbours and we even played some music.

I overheard several times, James' friends saying, "James would have loved this, all this fuss and attention."

This was comforting in a way but at the same time, I felt my heart literally aching for his presence. It seemed as though we were acting out a parody of a party and I found it very difficult to stay composed. I battled with a constant sense of expectation that James would come walking into the garden, smiling in his usual way. It seemed utterly wrong that he wasn't there.

One of the most bizarre moments was when the local free newspaper landed on the doormat and there, on the front page, was an article about James' death. The press had contacted us at the outset in a very heavy-handed manner and our police liaison officers advised us to prepare a press statement. This spared us from painful and insensitive interviewing. The newspaper was passed round with solemnity and curiously, for a moment, it felt as though James walked among us in the light of the afternoon.

James' friends expressed their feelings in a remembrance book, which was passed round the garden in the sunshine. I will never forget those glimpses of the girls, and some of the boys, taking the book into a quiet corner and sitting down, earnestly writing their thoughts.

One wrote: "I can't believe he's gone and he'll never be there again on a night out or one of those nights or days when I would sit down and talk to him, he was the easiest and best person to talk to. I just felt so close to him and I could open up to him and he would love to listen and wouldn't laugh."

Another girl said: "From the moment we met I knew we'd be friends forever, I've never had quite so much fun with one person. So many memories and so many laughs. A huge, huge part of me is missing now you're gone."
Still another wrote: "I'm sure one day I will understand why your time was so early but it does feel incredibly unfair. James, I'm going to miss you so much there will not be a day that passes where I won't think of you.... Love you always and with all my heart."

Although it is heart-rending to read such sentiments, I couldn't help but be proud that James made such an impression on his friends, and it would appear from several of the entries in the book that his friendships were immensely important to him. One friend said: "I can probably count on one hand the number of times I met you but you were such an amazing person; you made an impact."

31

It seems incredible to look back and remember that we managed to attend, a mere couple of days after James' funeral, a get together organised by his friends held at one of the pubs they used to visit. I have no idea how I managed to hold myself together, particularly when we arrived and saw an almost life size enlarged photo of James in pride of place in the bar. His friends told us that they wanted to remember James in a place he knew and enjoyed, and we all contributed to a local charity, turning the evening into a somewhat impromptu fundraising event. Many of James' favourite songs were played, his friends came and talked to us and shared their memories of him and it was a wonderful tribute organised by people who obviously rated him so highly.

Whilst the funeral may, to many of the mourners, make a death real and begin to bring some closure, for those who are closest it retains an air of unreality and it is only later that the finality of the proceedings can be absorbed.

It is really helpful to meet people who are following a similar grief path. In a way it validates that I am somehow doing this right. One such person, with whom I have tremendous empathy, is a woman called Linda. We met through the organisation that is run by bereaved parents, for bereaved parents; The Compassionate Friends (TCF), in 2009.

Linda wrote a moving piece in the TCF magazine that struck a chord with me and I contacted her via email. She lives locally and we discovered many parallels in our lives. Our first face-to-face meeting took place after a flurry of emails, at the RHS gardens in Wisley. Already recognising kindred spirits in each other, we walked and talked for hours! One of our immediate topics of discussion was, naturally, how our sons died and what happened in the aftermath. We observed many similarities in our reactions and emotions through that truly terrible time.

In June 2008, Linda's son Tom was travelling on a gap year adventure in Australia and New Zealand. He had arrived in New Zealand with the main aim of seeing the rugby match between England and the All Blacks. Funds were running short and he was offered some casual work in an orchard where two of his school friends, also travelling and whom he planned to meet, had secured temporary work.

Linda told me, "I had this awful dream in which I knew I was at a funeral and it was Tom's funeral. It was happening in a place with high, vaulted ceilings and sandstone walls. I woke up in a panic, unable to shake the dreadful feeling that something terrible had happened."

Linda checked her computer for emails and messages but there was nothing new; she convinced herself that everything was all right and set off for her work at a local school. Deep down she told me she still felt there was something wrong.

Later in the day, the police arrived at the school and Linda was told that Tom had lost his life in a quad bike accident on his first day working at the orchard.

"I can't describe," she said, "how it felt. The shock was so immense I couldn't take anything in.

My husband Ken somehow arrived, and it was all a blur after that, we had to go to tell Chris, Tom's brother who was at school, Gordon's School. The police took us. I remember telling Chris in the headmaster's study and Chris punching the wall.

Then they took us home, somehow; I don't even remember getting there. There was this awful whirl of people in and out of the house for days and the phone never stopped ringing. We had barely a minute to ourselves.

People kept turning up with food none of us could eat (why is it always mince – bolognaise or chilli?). We tried to decide if we should go to New Zealand, or not. We simply couldn't work out the logistics of who should go, who shouldn't go, all complicated by a huge time difference and so in the end we didn't go at all.

Our levels of functioning were all over the place. Whoever was strong enough at the time helped everyone else with whatever we needed to do in a practical sense.

I discovered the existence of international funeral directors who were in fact very good. They would arrange to repatriate Tom. Suddenly our beloved child was cargo. We had a moment that was almost farcical when the funeral directors increased their original quote to bring Tom home when they discovered he was six feet five inches tall. How such a thing could appear funny – of course it isn't but perhaps we needed the release of near-hysterical laughter at the time."

Gradually Linda and her husband Ken pieced together the tragedy that had happened, from various phone calls and emails and through speaking to Tom's two friends, Chris and James.

"They stayed with him after the accident. A helicopter came and airlifted Tom to hospital. His friends remained with him until he passed. I am so glad he was not alone. Of course, the fall out for them has been immense. They were all 19.

34

The next day they made commemorative T-shirts and went to the Ruby match. They felt Tom would have wanted them to do that. And I agree.

Time passed in the curious way of new bereavement, where some days feel endless and others seem to go by in a blink. We were always exhausted.

Tom was flown back to the UK about ten days after the accident."

Linda told me that Reverend Robinson, the Chaplain at Gordon's School, arranged for Tom's funeral to take place at Guildford Cathedral, partly because of his concern about finding a venue large enough to accommodate the numbers who would wish to attend.

In fact, on the day, Monday 30 June 2008, hundreds of mourners turned up to pay their respects to Tom. They were made up of family and friends new and old. Rugby players, workmates from Waitrose, teachers and school friends, his hairdresser and dentist and even his first nursery school teacher, all filed into the huge space of the Cathedral for the service. People travelled from as far away as Australia to be there and Linda was overwhelmed.

She added, "When I arrived at the Cathedral, I realised its significance. This was the place in my dream."

Linda and I (and other bereaved parents I have spoken with) all agree on one thing; The police, and other authorities (generally) seem ill equipped and ill-trained to deal with people in the immediate post loss period.

In Linda's case, the two police officers initially arrived at her home and actually imparted the awful news directly to her mother-in-law who shares the same surname.

Surely, they should have checked more carefully that they were dealing with the mother - not the grandmother - of a teenager? It seems incredible that they did not realise that the woman they initially met was of another generation.

Coroner's officers must by the nature of their work need to have a pragmatic and dispassionate attitude, but to refer to your beloved son as "the corpse" is both unnecessary and distressing. The local undertakers seem to have the most empathy. In fact, the undertakers for Linda's son have a tradition of giving bereaved mothers a red rose in recognition of their loss.

Perhaps there should be liaison courses across the board for the authorities to improve the general level of awareness and training in imparting the worst possible news to parents. Their main concern currently seems to be to tell the family as quickly as possible and remove themselves from the situation.

Our society today has created an environment that expects the grieving process to be over quickly so that life can move on, just like a soap opera. I remember feeling very flat and depressed after the funeral was over. Suddenly there were no more arrangements to be made; there was nothing to plan for in relation to James. The phone became quiet at last and the outside world, utterly heedless, carried on as normal. I remember thinking that it seemed so unfair that the sun could still shine, the dawn still hold such promise of the day to come, when my son was dead.

If one supposes we are holistic beings made up of a trinity of mind, body and spirit, then it is fair to say that all three elements of that trinity are severely affected by such traumatic loss. My mind was like cotton wool and my intelligence was blunted. My body was weary; some days even putting one foot in front of the other was a mammoth effort. My sleep pattern was disturbed – in fact it has never really recovered.

Early on, Shaun and I both found that our appetites varied from an intense desire for food and drink at regular intervals throughout the day, to a complete absence of appetite and the normal anticipation of eating.

The first few months after James died consisted of eating to live rather than living to eat. It was a long while before we had any wish to dine out in a restaurant for pleasure.

My emotions were shaken up into an all pervading numbness alternating with a hunger for affection.

Sometimes all I wanted was for Shaun to hold me tight, other times I barely wanted him near me. I found that when we went out I would link arms with him or hold his hand, I literally didn't want to let him out of my sight and I found mundane places like supermarkets and shopping centres could induce a sense of anxiety and panic in me. I found it difficult to shop alone and avoided local stores so as not to encounter people whom I knew.

The return of intimacy to our relationship was a gradual process that we had to work at. I recall Shaun saying at one point that we needed to cleave together for the strength to get through this terrible time, and I am sure he was right.

I felt as though I had lost all my usual terms of reference on how to behave.

I returned to work fairly soon after the funeral but I do not imagine I was functioning normally. My colleagues were very kind and shielded me from all but the most important telephone calls. My office is located in such a position that I could come into work unobserved and I did not have to meet many other people and make small talk, which was very important at the time, as I didn't know how I would feel from one minute to the next.

I got up every day, carried out my usual rituals of showering, putting on makeup and doing my hair, but it all felt unreal, like I was half a step behind everyone else. I am sure this is not uncommon and this too was the time I felt that I learned to don the mask of the grieving parent. It went on with my makeup and came off again when I went to bed at night. I became accustomed to the sick feeling in the pit of my stomach that hit me anew every morning when I awoke, and realised that it really had happened, it really was true that James died. I lived with that feeling for a very long time before it dissipated. In the early days, weeks and months following loss, time took on a strange quality.

The days – and nights – dragged that summer, yet suddenly we were in late September and I had no real sense of how time had passed.

One Saturday, Shaun and I went to Wisley. This has long been a favourite place that we visit through the seasons. I had last been there shortly before James' death.
We followed our usual route, which took in the main avenue of summer borders – twin, large borders either side of a grassy pathway, which are always splendid in summer.

"Oh no!" I exclaimed, dismayed. "How did that happen? All the flowers have gone over."

I was so upset to see that the buds, which I had seen shortly before James's death, were now gone, spent and brown, dried and desiccated on their stems with the onset of early autumn. I felt cheated, deprived of my customary sense of the progression of the seasons.

"Is this how it is going to be, then?" I demanded of Shaun, "Not noticing what is around us because of what has happened to us personally? It is awful, dreadful, unbearable…"

I remember this as one of the lowest moments I experienced and it emphasised how different life would be for us now. Shaun comforted me as best as he could but he was equally upset to realise we were subject to such a profound change.

One of the most common grief reactions is anger. Yet I never felt angry with James for what had happened. His death was a stupid, preventable accident. But how could I feel anger at what had befallen him? Rather, I felt a sense of bewilderment that a set of circumstances had come together and seemingly conspired to take my son away from me. I asked myself many questions in those early days, particularly wondering why, as a parent, I had not been allowed to keep both my children. It really felt as though James had been stolen away from me at a point in my life where, newly remarried, I was rediscovering true happiness. But when I analysed whether anger played a part in my grief, or not, I questioned where exactly I could direct my anger.

Certainly not to James, who took a bad decision that denied him his life; certainly not to the friends who were with him that night. I have always emphasised that I do not blame them or hold any of them accountable *in any way* for what happened to James. I suppose I could be angry with the planners of the nightclub who sited it on the riverside with scant regard for the safety of the customers.

I suppose I could be angry with the bouncers of the nightclub for not ensuring late night revellers were turned towards the town rather than the river.

I suppose I could be angry with the licensed trade for making alcohol so cheap it was easy for James and his peers to get drunk without spending much money.

I suppose I could be angry with the Fates for allowing this particular falling of the runes.

In the end, I realised it is impossible to hold anyone accountable for another person's actions, even if those actions are impaired and unintentional.

I realised that anger would not serve any purpose. I think I would have felt differently if James had died at the hand of another, but because his passing was accidental, it is impossible to lay blame at any particular door.

Positive emotions are uplifting; negative emotions are not, and I am glad that I was able to feel this way.

Once James' funeral service had been held, I knew that I would be turning to focus my energies onto a campaign with Kingston Council and this would require all my concentration. I also knew it would not serve me to be sidelined by anger at this time.

Any resentment that I felt was directed at the authorities that had allowed the situation at Kingston to exist for such a long time without taking action, particularly as lives had previously been lost in the river.

Memory

Remember me
But do not put your lives on hold
Weave me into the fabric of new normality
And learn that I celebrate immortality

Remember me
Draw with joy the spectrum of our moments
Paint me with the palette of your days
And believe that I am in the better place

Remember me
When you wake tearful in dawn's light
Be brushed by the balm of my presence
And trust in my easy calm existence

Remember me
Gather and hold the colours of my love
Across your heart; stitch my rainbow daily
And accept I walk with you for eternity.

Andrea Corrie, 2005

Chapter 3

Meet the New Woman

"Healing doesn't mean never experiencing pain; it means learning to live with the pain, learning to live without the physical presence of your child and learning to find some enjoyment again."

Jan Andersen

It is difficult to be objective about ourselves. Losing a child necessarily engenders a great deal of introspection as one tries, and at first generally fails, to make some kind of sense of what has happened and to absorb just how it changes you as a person. You are living through unimaginably difficult soul-crushing devastation. How on earth can you come out the other side?

There is, for myself, an irrefutable fact. The Andrea whom I was on 27 July 2005 became somebody else by the end of 28 July 2005. Still Andrea, but altered, changed, and never to return to being the 27 July version.

There is no choice but to continue life after such a loss, however hard that is.

Libby Purves, a writer and broadcaster who lost her son to suicide, wrote [1]"There is no solution to grief. Somebody had a metaphor for bereavement.

'You go through a long tunnel, sometimes very dark, sometimes broad with glass roofs, but you're still in it, you're always going to be in it, because it happened.'

This is the truth of being bereaved. How cruel a truth...And yet, without moving forward to take this truth on board, you cannot reasonably expect to be able to live a meaningful existence."

I recall that in the early days, I resented the fact that sun and earth carried on rotating, the birds still sang, the plants still grew. How dare the world continue, heedless and uncaring, whilst we had to fight through shock and disbelief? But now I am better able to understand and even draw comfort from the normality, even banality, of everyday life going on around me. If the world had stopped turning on that fateful day, I would surely be in a darker place now. As humans, we are designed to care, to feel pain, to hurt when something bad happens. It would be a sterile and loveless world if we were without emotion.

Initially, James' passing left me feeling unbalanced, lopsided. I had two children, an even pair. I had been blessed with one girl and one boy. I counted my blessings to have two beautiful, healthy, lively intelligent individuals who filled me with pride with all their achievements, large and small.

I am no saint, and of course like any family we had tiffs and arguments, but these were always within the parameters of our loving relationship.

My children knew I loved them and vice versa. We are quite a demonstrative family and shared an easy affection.

[1, 2] First published in *The Daily Mail*, 20 April 2009

Throughout their formative years, through nursery, pre-school, school, Brownies, Cubs, St John's Ambulance, Scouts, Duke of Edinburgh Award schemes and the myriad activities carried out by children as they progress through their young lives, I was happy to be mum to Stella and James.

But who am I after the cataclysm that occurred on 28 July 2005?

Well, I am *still* Stella and James' mum and along the way I have become stepmum to Shaun's children, Mark and Janine. We have moved into the wonderful realms of being grandparents with the birth of Janine's gorgeous little girl, Madelaine, and becoming a grandmother is indeed a source of great joy.

My mother died in 2001 and my father in 2003, yet I still consider myself to be a daughter. In the same way, although I have lost one of my children, I still do and always will, consider myself to be the mother of two children, a son and a daughter. I am a sister to my brother and an aunt to my nephew.

I experienced other forms of grief through separation and divorce in 1999 and the subsequent death of my ex-husband who died in 2002. I am not sure whether I ever felt like a widow in the accepted sense; it is a strange kind of limbo when one is divorced, yet grief exists for the lost marriage and the death of my ex-spouse. After all, we loved each other enough to create children together and that has never been diminished by the subsequent breakdown of our marriage. I have never regretted having my children. When their father died, we pulled together to work through the loss.

I had to set aside the negative feelings associated with the divorce which was, after all, fairly recent, but somehow the three of us, Stella, James and I, managed to meld together and work through the worst of this very difficult time.

In the early days of my grief for James, I felt as though my identity had disappeared beneath the weight of my loss. Mentally I groped in the dark to find myself. I felt as though there was no such thing as normality. Outward normality was simply a mask behind which I concealed my sorrow.

Actually I felt as though I cared little what happened to me; my thoughts were focused on getting through the days in some semblance of normality – if I am honest, to try and be normal for everyone else. I do not think that initially I gave much thought to the 'ego of self' at that time. Early grief is very introspective but it is not particularly analytical. I did not have the energy at the time to evaluate how I actually felt; it was enough of a struggle to get through the waking hours.

The sense of loss in the early days of grieving was so acute that it coloured my every waking moment and I felt as though it must show in my face. Indeed, when I look at photos taken during the first year or two, I see myself looking pinched and pale; certainly my smile does not reach my eyes. I look like someone who is bearing a burden.

Grief is a dark place that can feel like an underground cave.

The blank, dark walls of the cave are at first easier to study than the light surroundings of normal life.

But gradually, I began to emerge. It is hard to say which was more painful at that point; embracing the light of the life that went on around me or remaining in the darkness of my grief.

As time passed, I began to spend more and more time above the ground. I began to start needing the light more than I needed the darkness.

Today I can say that I live in the light again, but sometimes, even now, grief will come out of nowhere and floor me, and I will go scurrying for the security of the cave; but more often than not, I will only visit for a brief time. I no longer need to live out of the light.

I have learned to accept that grief is a process, not an event. It has a beginning but not an ending. It becomes part of the fabric of self and cannot be removed.

I have learned that I needed to stay in that cave early on in my grief, and I want to stay out of the cave now.

I have learned that it is important to let the journey unfold in its own way and accept it as it is; not to question it or to try to make it what I thought, or what others thought, it should be.

I have learned that it is helpful for me to reach out to others who are struggling with grief, through the voice of my writing.

I have learned the skills that allow me to treat others with various complementary therapies; focusing on other people and their troubles, should they wish to share them, gives a different and more balanced perspective on my grief.

47

I have learned that I have moved slowly from a dark place to a light place and I am thankful to walk into the place that I think of as the mourning light. The mourning light is not quite the same as the 'before bereavement' light, but it is pretty close. It is true that grief itself dims with time but the light inside us that is the essence of our spirit and our being continues to shine brighter and brighter until it is able to break through the darkness.

I asked my dear friend Pauline, also known as my 'Yorkshire sister' because we are so close, and whom I have known since Stella and James were very young, how she perceives that I have changed since James died. She said,

"I remember getting that phone call from Andrea when James had not returned home from that fateful night out. Of course, although we were both concerned, neither of us expected the dreadful news that was to come.

As mothers, pictures whizzed through our minds. Over the time between James going missing and him being found we spoke every few hours, just to touch base. I had to be there to support my friend even though she had Shaun. We have been friends for years and have 'been there' for each other over many sad times. When the awful call came to say that James had been found in the river I cried … It was unbelievable. To say I felt Andrea's pain would be untrue. How can one fully understand when one doesn't walk in another's shoes? Yes, I felt real sympathy, sadness, and my own personal pain, but I could never feel what it was like for Andrea, Shaun and Stella.

I knew how much Andrea loved her children. She was a good mother, realising, as most of us do, that our children are not angels, but trying to give them guidelines in life.

My usually sensible, 'together', well organised friend fell apart. I needed to be close to her to give her my support, but as I had moved away from the area this had to be by telephone, not physical. We talked many times in those early days. How on earth do you make sense of such a tragedy?

To say I was amazed at the way Andrea was handling things would be an understatement. I travelled down to the funeral. I needed to be there for my friend almost as much as for myself. I remember all those faces at the crematorium. Many I recognised, but far more I didn't. I managed to sit behind Andrea and remember putting my hand on her shoulder to let her know I was there. It hurt me badly to see the pain she was in. I needed to help in any way I could.

We talked a lot over those early weeks. We laughed at things James used to do. We both had very strong feelings that he was still around. Little things happened. Odd things. He wasn't far away. He still isn't. The most important thing I felt I could do was to just be there at the other end of the phone line whenever Andrea wanted to talk or cry. We had many phone calls at all sorts of hours where she sobbed and I silently cried. My part in all this was just to try and be normal (well, as normal as I can be). To talk about James. Some people don't know what to say following a death of anyone let alone a child, but I knew how important it was to Andrea to talk about James. He lived. Why not speak of him? He touched many people. For one so young he had made quite an impact on many lives so why not talk about him? Laugh. He had a naughty sense of humour so would appreciate us laughing.

Gradually, my old friend started to show herself again. Her campaign to get railings along the river bank where James was lost helped a lot as does her writing. I never cease to be amazed at Andrea's strength and with this she has developed a new empathy with other people. Families who have lost that someone special. The groups she has joined have helped her share the worst experience of her life and in this she has also been able to help others.

I am aware in writing this that I haven't said anything about Stella and Shaun.

They have lived this experience with Andrea. I am so proud of the way they have all pulled together and helped support each other.

They are all amazing. James would be proud too of the way they have dealt with such a dreadful happening. Something positive out of such devastation."

One of the worst things about being bereaved is that other people no longer know how to treat you. I found myself, fairly early on drawing on some hitherto unexplored acting ability. People do not want to see you weeping and wailing. They want to see you as they expect to see you; they want to see you as far as possible like you used to be. This is a pretty tall order!

It is never wise to ask a bereaved person how he or she is feeling unless you really want to hear the answer. Sometimes we may just say we are 'doing all right' or 'OK' but if you catch us at the wrong moment, we may well release quite a tirade. I am afraid that unpredictability of personality goes with the territory of being bereaved and especially in the early days, this can be difficult to control.

It was not long before I found that I could project a normal persona, with which other people felt safe and comfortable. It seemed that others were much happier to be around me if they weren't expecting me to dissolve into tears at the slightest provocation. But the downside of this turned out to be that I did such a good job of suppressing my grief, that it accumulated inside me like steam in a pressure cooker.

I know better now that it has to come out somehow and the device that I used several times in the first year was not a very good one. I would wait until Shaun was asleep and creep downstairs, arm myself with a bottle of wine, a pack of cigarettes, and the telephone. I would skulk at the end of the garden where no-one could hear me, phone the Samaritans and weep and wail drunkenly down the phone for a bit.

I felt terribly ashamed of behaving this way; in fact more than once I rang and apologised to the Samaritans for my rants, in the cold light of day, but fortunately they were terribly understanding and for me, doing this helped me to express my grief. However, given the remorse I felt for behaving, as I saw it, so badly, I would not recommend this as a good way of letting out grief!

I no longer smoke and my alcohol intake does not include late night sessions in the garden these days. It may not have been an ideal way to deal with the release of the burden but it worked for me, although I would emphasise this was only in the short term and I am only speaking of a handful of occasions. It still feels like a guilty secret, though.

These experiences served to underline for me one of the most fundamental truths of grief. It simply cannot be sidelined, however strong and resilient a person you are.

It was probably not until year three or so that I felt I was beginning to live life again, as opposed to just going through the motions. Early grief is very selfish, or perhaps self-absorbed is a better way to describe it. I needed a great deal of thinking time to try to absorb the enormity of the loss, and I was so lucky during this time to have a great deal of support around me. I was able to coast at work, through the help of my colleagues, and if I felt anti-social I could creep into the office via a back door route and not have to communicate. At home, Shaun has always given me the space that I need just to be with my grief.

I like the positivity of drawing on analogies of the way in which grief changes with time, and I particularly like the following, which was posted on the online TCF forum: "Instead of us hoping our grief would become smaller (i.e. a circle) it always stayed the same size. What happened was another circle grew bigger round the circle of grief (which for so long is and has to be the only experience we have)."

I use this as a visualisation. As time has passed I have moved from being totally grief stricken to where I am today. I visualise my grief for my child as constant, yet a new life has grown round it. The new life is calmer but still there are times when the onslaught of grief can totally floors me, but as time passes the recovery is much quicker.

I visualise an ever increasing area of the new circle of life yet the original circle of grief remains the same. On my bad days, I 'see' I am fully back in the circle of grief but have to hold onto the knowledge that I won't stay there."
This is a good way to express the way in which life can and does move forward following cataclysmic loss.

In terms of how I view my own personality, I believe myself to be a warmer, more compassionate and less intolerant woman than my pre loss self. I have taken courses in complementary therapies and these have proved invaluable in giving me back confidence and self esteem. It is interesting that the majority of healers and people who move into teaching in the therapy field have been driven by some kind of trauma or life changing event; it certainly seems to trigger something different in the pace at which we live our lives.

Another friend whom I met through TCF has become a trained and qualified healer since she lost her son, also in 2005. During one of our email exchanges she told me, "We have all this love to give, that we can't physically and in the present heap upon our boys any more. I have to do something with it and it seems to me logical to share it around to benefit others in the best way I can."

'Time is a great healer' – the cliché is familiar but I would regard it as true, to a certain extent. The tearing agony of early grief gives way to an ever present, dull, background ache that sits somewhere alongside my heartbeat, but I couldn't put a time scale on its evolution from rawness to something akin to an acceptable level of pain. Doctors are fond of scoring pain on a scale of one to ten, and at first I would have said my grief was ten and higher, but today it sits at around two or three with the occasional peak to five or six before dropping back again.

I often feel sorry for my husband Shaun because I am not the woman he married. I remember saying to him soon after we lost James, "The day we got married was the best day of my life. The day we lost James, a scant six weeks later, was the worst day of my life and it was the day that the Andrea you knew and married died too."

53

Shaun is amazing because he loves the new me as much as the old me. I am indeed lucky to have such support.

Libby Purves goes on to refer to the Anglo-Saxon origin of the word 'accept'. [2]"It means 'picking up the thread.' You go on weaving your life because you have no choice."

She says, "I have now had nearly three years without a son. Miseries have happened, happinesses have happened, you go on weaving. There's nothing else you can do."

People around you, those you thought you knew, see you as a changed person, too. They no longer see you, they see a bereaved parent. I believe this is similar to the way people with a terminal illness are perceived - no longer that person, but that person with the illness. It is interesting to remember that before we ourselves were bereaved parents, we probably would have behaved in exactly the same way to the newly bereaved; shuffling our feet and not knowing what to say.

It is only our own unwelcome experience that gives us the insight that we did not formerly have, which should make us a little more accepting of the way we are treated.

The first time I began a friendship that was not initiated through shared loss, I felt it was a good validation of progress in grief.

By this I mean that I was not perceived as a bereaved parent; the new friendship had nothing to do with grief and loss and it felt like a massive step forward. Initially it feels quite normal to tell everyone about your loss, but these days I am far more selective. It is a terrible conversation stopper when you are in a social group, say at a party, and someone asks you about your children.

54

I have to decide on the spot what to say. I always acknowledge James in some way but I will deflect conversation onto the other person's family or speak about something else. I do not feel guilty for doing this – although I think I would have done earlier on – because to a great extent it is self preservation not to want to share intimate details with strangers in a social situation.

There are a variety of answers to the dreaded question, "And how many children do you have?" I find the easiest response to be "Two, and two step-children. How about you?" If I were to reply, "A daughter, two step-children and a son (but he is no longer with us)…." I know the response would be an awkward silence, which would then invite me to explain my response. Sometimes it is all too wearing to contemplate.

Last year I was at a wedding and one of the guests approached me. She said she remembered me from where I used to work about 12 years ago. I was gratified that she recognised me, particularly when she exclaimed, "You haven't changed a bit; I would have known you anywhere!"

This was a positive confirmation for me that these days, my loss is not written on my face.

Equally because this was someone who knew me before my loss, it was easier to tell her that we had lost James, without awkward embarrassment, as naturally enough, she asked after my children.

I am comfortable in my own skin now. I have learned to accept that I cannot have my old life back in any form, as the substance of it was fragmented the day we lost James.

It may seem strange to say but although I like the person I am now, I wish I could have become that person without experiencing our loss.

One of the greatest lessons for me in grief, has been learning to assimilate a new and different personal world and this takes a degree of personal courage. I like the way this is illustrated in this Native American blessing from the 1800s:

"Go Forward with Courage
When you are in doubt, be still, and wait;
When doubt no longer exists for you,
Then go forward with courage.
So long as mists envelop you, be still;
Be still until the sunlight pours through and dispels the mists
...as it surely will.
Then act with courage"

Bereaved parents are often looked upon as brave for coping with their loss. I don't think it is necessarily bravery that keeps us going. Rather, it is a dogged determination not to let what has happened beat us. It takes a great deal of effort and application to get through the entire grieving process. Courage, bravery, pluck, mettle, nerve, purpose, tenacity, fortitude, are all words that can be applied to those who are struggling to maintain a normal life after loss. I have not encountered any grieving parents who say they cannot dig out some sort of reserves to help them along the grief path.

In the early days, it is tempting to give in, pull up the duvet and close out the world, but this does eventually pass and the time between feeling the depths of despair gradually stretches out – from hours, to days, to weeks.

I would not say that I have yet reached a point where I do not have some low days so I have not expanded that timespan to months.

Stress in grieving is difficult to quantify. Are you stressed because you are grieving or is your grief making you stressed? The two things are so closely linked it is impossible to separate them and maybe this is where therapy, perhaps in the form of counselling, can be very helpful. Certainly in the early stages of grieving, stress seems to be magnified as though life is moving in slow motion and everything, from small decisions to large, is tougher than usual. This is countered by lack of interest, lethargy and overwhelming tiredness that renders the most mundane tasks almost insurmountable.

There is an ever present stress particularly in early grief when it is an enormous effort to present a 'normal' persona to the outside world. I found I could resist tears and behave very well in the hardest hours of my grief most of the time. But then, if someone gave me a friendly wave, or spoke to me kindly, I could be undone by their small kindnesses and it would take not only them, but myself by surprise.

The good news is that the negative embodiments of your stress and grief will eventually pass and it is possible to regain a semblance of normality in day to day life.

One of the best stress-busters is learning how to control reactions to stress and understand how to create a pattern that helps you as an individual. Most of us spend a great deal of time being active in other people's lives and create for ourselves roles where we are great helpers. In grieving, it is important to put yourself first and, as the saying goes, put on your own oxygen mask before you help someone else with theirs.

When you are able to focus on your self and help your own self, you are much better able to help others.

The courage of being able to put up your hands, recognise your need and say: "I need some help now, I simply can't go any further without it" is the true bravery of grief. When you are a grieving parent you spend a lot of time being strong for everyone around you, but this may not ultimately help your own strength and ability to deal with your grief.

Stress in grief manifests itself in a variety of ways, some of them more unexpected than others. I found that I developed a hyper anxiety about my family and friends. If I could not get hold of Shaun on the phone during the day, for example, I would get into a panic very quickly. My mind would run riot, imagining all sorts of dreadful fates befalling him. It was ridiculous in terms of cold logic, because he is often on the road and frequently cannot get a phone signal or he is driving and misses my calls, but the anxiety I felt was out of all proportion. He would be dismayed to have his head bitten off when he eventually called me back and ultimately I had to explain that every time I failed to get in touch with him, it was another stress for me to take on board.

Stella and I developed a similar high level of anxiety about each other. In some ways, I suppose it was easier because she was already living over 200 miles from home, so I was accustomed to not hearing from her for days on end, but when James first died, we both felt we needed the reassurance of knowing that the other was as all right as we could be. It took a long time for us to lengthen the gap between our calls or emails.

It is an aspect of grief that we have discussed and we both agreed that the need to know each other's whereabouts was and remains very important to both of us.

Sometimes simple things can be great stress busters. First, you must give yourself permission to take time out. Then you have to take that time to do something that you want to do...not what others want you to do or what you think you should do. As parents, we are already conditioned to put ourselves second after the family, but in grief there should be the opportunity for you to say, "This is my time now, and I am going to take it and enjoy it."

Exercise, cooking a meal, visiting the library, watching an old film on TV – really anything that takes you away from the constant thoughts of grief are all good positive stress relievers.

It is true to say that negativity feeds upon itself to drag you down and positivity spirals you upwards. My spiritual path has taught me to focus on my self – not the self of ego, but the holistic aspects of mind, body and spirit, which begin with a focus on breathing, the very essence of life.

Before losing James my knowledge of such things was minimal but I have discovered that the relaxation techniques taught, for example through yoga and Pilates, are immensely helpful in stilling the mind chatter, which distracts us from simply being. We lead such busy lives and put ourselves under such pressure to always be doing things, we can lose the ability to take time out from that and just be.

Shaun is a good example of how to process stress. He may not get to do it as regularly as he would wish but from time to time he goes fishing. This involves an inordinately time-consuming process of loading up his car with a number of essential items (rods, nets, floats etc). He takes a packed lunch and sets off early in the morning to a small local fishing lake where he chooses his pitch and there he sits for the day.

Over the course of the day he will catch some fish, which are humanely put back into the water. But really, the day isn't about the number or size of the fish he catches.

He comes home from a fishing day tired, usually sunburned and happy and tells me of the birds he has seen, the peace and tranquillity he has enjoyed, but most of all he delights in being able to switch off from all our day to day stress-inducing intrusions.

There is much focus on post traumatic stress disorder in grief and how it manifests itself. To a degree I wonder whether all bereaved parents have a degree of PTSD because child loss is so traumatic, whether it is anticipated or totally unexpected, whether it is a baby, a child, teenager or adult.

Clinical depression may also result from the stress associated with grief, as can anxiety syndrome and panic attacks, and all these manifestations of stress require medical help. We are often reluctant to admit we cannot cope, being too ready to struggle on in our own way without accepting the need for aid.

I was fortunate to have a supportive GP who monitored me in the early days to ensure that I was not manifesting adverse symptoms, and it is worth bearing in mind if you are supporting someone who is newly bereaved that they may be suffering from a clinical disorder requiring treatment.

In jest, I would describe myself as having been as "mad as a box of frogs" during the first year or so of grieving, but it was probably not that far from the truth! The trauma of losing a child is such a profoundly stressful event that no-one could ever hope to escape unscathed mentally. It is the ways in which you learn to channel your stress, grief and anguish that in the end lead to the resurgence of your (almost) intact persona. But I make no apologies for the sweeping statement that grief cannot fail to make a different person of you; it is simply not possible to be exactly the person you were before.

You are not You

You are the one who stands beside me through the days
The one whom at times I will visit and never forget
The one who listens in my heart as I speak
And the one who lights my way through darkness.
You are the one who forgives my descent into anger
The one who lifts my spirits to a smile
The one who comprehends my mellowing grief
And the one who absorbs my sorrow
You are the one who encourages me to walk forward
The one who gives strength to my every breath
The one who shows me the beauty in the days
And the one who colours my sleep with dreams.
You are the one who makes me rise like a phoenix
From the ashes of my despair
The one who lovingly guides my life's journey
And the one who will greet me, when I arrive.

Inspired by the poem 'I am not I' but Juan Ramon Jimenez

Chapter 4

Would You Like to Talk About It?

How would you respond if you were invited to speak to a group of trained and trainee Cruse counsellors about living with the loss of your child? I was invited to address such a group in October 2010, just over five and years after James died.

I was asked to speak to a group in my local area as part of the Cruse Bereavement Care Training Programme for Surrey, South East England.

Cruse is a registered charity that offers a specialist website, and telephone, email and face-to-face support for adults, children and young people who are grieving. The organisation's website describes grief in necessarily general terms, saying: "The length of time it will take a person to accept the death of someone close and move forward is varied and will be unique to the mourner.

No-one can tell you how or when the intensity of your grief will lessen; only you will know when this happens. It is not unusual for bereaved people to think they are finally moving towards acceptance only to experience the strong and often unwelcome emotions they experienced shortly after the death.

Life will never be the same again after bereavement, but the grief and pain should lessen. There should come a time when you are able to adapt, adjust, and cope with life without the person who has died. The pain of bereavement has been compared to that of losing a limb. We may adapt to life without the limb but we continue to feel its absence.

When a person we are close to dies, we can find meaning in life again, but without forgetting their meaning for us.

Many people worry that they will forget the person who has died; how they looked, their voice, or the good times they had together."

My own contact with Cruse began some eight months after James died, and my sessions were invaluable. I made initial contact simply through looking up the number of our local branch.

I took the option of having the counsellor visit me in my own home and having sessions on familiar ground certainly helped in allowing me to express my grief in a safe, controlled manner.

My counselling period represented a significant step on the way to my beginning to understand the path my life would take following the loss of my son, and how I could achieve my own progress, as I saw it.

Initially I was so defensive about the need for counselling that the counsellor later told me she felt as though she was talking to me through a glass wall in our early sessions. I must have been quite a challenge!

I held the view that it was rather self-indulgent to sit and talk to someone else about feelings and emotions surrounding an event. This was undoubtedly an opinion formed through my own ignorance, and having never been in a situation where I felt a need for counselling.

Thus, when the counsellor first arrived, I remember feeling affronted when she tried to draw me on my feelings and emotions. I recall that our first session did not go particularly well as her questions felt intrusive.

I was particularly indignant when she asked me, "Do you feel you have said goodbye to James?"

It seemed a particularly insensitive question. I retorted angrily that I would never feel I had said goodbye to my son, for that would mean an ending to our relationship, or that I no longer thought about him.

However, on further discussion I understood that the counsellor was asking me whether I accepted the *reality* of James' passing because I had not seen him since he left the house fit well and full of life, three days before he was found. Looking back, I don't think I ever had a problem accepting that he was no longer alive ... but perhaps I did. It was in fact years before I could use the word 'died' rather than any other alternative, such as 'passed away', 'gone to the other side', etc, to describe his not being here.

Gradually, I came to realise how helpful it was to be able to speak of James, to speak of my anguish surrounding the loss, and my fears on an everyday level at being able to cope and re-form my life after such cataclysmic loss. I was able to voice my innermost thoughts to the counsellor without fear of criticism or reprisal and it was a good freedom. She was non-judgemental and became a great help to me in clarifying my own thoughts and beliefs surrounding my loss.

She helped me to see that though counselling is beneficial, in the end recovery is an individual process that cannot be achieved by someone else on your behalf. It is something that you simply must do for yourself.

I recently wrote to ask her how she viewed me now as opposed to when we first met in the counselling sessions. She replied:

"As I didn't know Andrea before James' death I can't comment on what the old Andrea was like. What I can tell you is that the Andrea I met at the start of our sessions together was very different to the woman she is today.

As Cruse Bereavement Care, we primarily go to people's homes where the sessions take place. When I turned up for our first session, I expected to meet a grieving person in despair, somebody whose world had been turned upside down, it is not often I have met somebody quite as spiky. She made it plain that she didn't know how talking could possibly help, but we decided to give it a go anyway.

Andrea was at that point, in my opinion, a black or white person, and the new Andrea today embraces all the different shades of grey plus all the colours of the rainbow.

Through our sessions, I witnessed Andrea slowly giving up control, stop fighting, take the mask off and allow herself to become vulnerable. I have seen a woman slowly rebuild her life and then some; to witness a person deciding to live life to the fullest instead of opting only to exist, is a privilege. She has never gone for the safe option but has challenged herself all the way. Helping others has been one of the keys to her recovery through her writing, supporting other bereaved parents, her work as a complementary therapist and public speaking.

Today there is a spark in her eyes, a sense of mischievous joy, an appreciation of life but also of her precious memories of her beloved son James – her perfect short story."

Any helping mechanisms, be they counselling, therapy, reading, spiritual practice or anything else, are merely tools in the armoury for recovery.

Soon after James died, I read the words of a bereaved mother, quoted on the forum of TCF who said, "When I myself get to the pearly gates - hopefully not for a long time yet - and I am reunited with my son, he will ask me, 'Well mum, what have you been doing all these years, since I died?' I do not want to answer, 'Why son, I haven't been doing anything very much. I have just been grieving for you!' What I will tell him is, 'Well son, although I missed you as though my heart would break, I carried on living my life as fully as I could, so that when I got to meet up with you again, I would have plenty to tell you about all our lives after you had left us.'"

This gave me a seminal message about grief and grieving, and I was so grateful at the time to read something *positive* that a parent could say about her loss. Hence, after some consideration and thought, I decided to go ahead with the talk for the Cruse counsellors, because I felt that James would approve, and, after all, I would be telling his story. It is rare to find a bereaved parent who doesn't like to use their child's name in conversation and talk about his or her life.

Thus, I agreed that I would address the group. I was uncertain what I, and the audience, could expect from the session. However, I found it helpful to prepare cue cards with words or phrases that would prompt me, set out in chronological sequence so that if nerves or emotion got the better of me, I would be able to steer myself back on track. I have little experience of public speaking, and my main concern was that I would get flustered or upset and be unable to convey my message clearly.

The day duly arrived. I felt very nervous and although I was given the opportunity to pull out, even at this late stage, I knew there was value in what I was doing and by this point I felt I could not possibly let everyone down, including myself.

The hardest part was visualising just how I would begin my address. I found it impossible to plan, as the audience began to gather in the room around me. I decided to leave it to Providence!

The audience numbered twenty-seven. Twenty-seven pairs of curious eyes observed me as the clock ticked round to the start time, seven o'clock. I figuratively pulled a protective cloak around myself and tried to project a calm, relaxed and confident persona.

The person introducing me merely stated: "This is Andrea and she is going to tell us about her son James, who died when he was 19."

At this there was there was a slight but audible, collective intake of breath. Thankfully I did not have to stand up to speak, and clasping my nervous palms together under the table, I took a deep breath and started to speak.

I began by relating how I thought I knew grief, having lost my mother in 2001, my ex husband in 2002 and my father in 2003. These were three separate and individual types of grief.

I did not undergo counselling for any of these losses, although with hindsight it may well have helped me with the feelings of loss and anger that I experienced. When my mother died, I was angry that such a dear person had suffered so much, as she had a torrid time in hospital with several operations for previously undetected Crohn's disease. It was an extremely difficult period for us; mum and dad lived in Cornwall and the frequent trips to and from the hospital when she was ill were exhausting. My father needed a great deal of support also and after mum died, he never recovered his zest for life.

When my ex husband died suddenly, this too was a dreadful shock for Stella, James and I. We had been divorced for three years and the children had an amicable relationship with him. I did not handle his passing well. I still held residual anger towards him over our divorce, and his death compounded this. I am sure that it sounds selfish, but I felt angry that I was left with all the responsibility for our children. Stella and James were marvellously supportive throughout the divorce period; it had come as a shock to them that their father and I were no longer living compatibly but we had formed a very cohesive unit.

It is interesting to me that when I had counselling after James died, I was able to revisit the feelings surrounding my divorce and the loss of my children's father and finally lay to rest the negativity and anger from that time.

My father died a scant three months after my ex husband, and I regret to say I do not think I have ever grieved properly for dad. He was so unhappy after he lost his dear Dorothy that there was a sense of relief that he was reunited with her with his passing. It seemed impossible to get beyond awful events at that time. However, such was our resilience that we made it.

After that, life settled down and in 2005 I married my dear husband Shaun. Everyone was so happy for us; Stella, James, and Mark and Janine.

Six weeks later, when Shaun and I were just beginning to relax into the happiness of our new married life, we had the incredibly traumatic shock of losing James.

I can hardly begin to describe the emotional rollercoaster of being ecstatically happy in June, and utterly devastated in July.

One of the worst aspects initially was a complete inability to absorb what had happened or indeed, to make any kind of sense of what felt like a living nightmare."

Once my talk was under way, I realised that the audience were listening attentively, and I began to grow confident enough to look up and at times make eye contact with some of them.

I realised that Stella's observation when I had told her about my planned address was wise. She had told me, "Well mum, you could hardly have a better audience, since they are trained to be non judgemental." This was very reassuring to a novice speaker.

I went on to describe my individual approach to grief and how it has evolved over time. Using the cue cards gave some helpful structure to what I said. I tried to convey the distinctly separate aspects that have helped me to work through such a horrendously shocking event and I spoke of what I call the three Ps:

"Proactivity – For me it was very important, as soon as James died, to find other people who truly understood what it was like to be a bereaved parent. To this end, I used the internet to find appropriate links to TCF and Drowning Support Network which have both in their own ways provided, and indeed continue to provide, a great deal of support.

I also looked for counselling and Cruse Bereavement Care was mentioned by my local GP. I contacted my local branch of Cruse, and waited some three to four months until an appropriate counsellor was available. I had specifically requested a counsellor who understood what it was to lose someone to water, because I felt it was essential for whoever counselled me to have some insight into this particular type of loss.

Positivity – From the outset I believe that it helped me to look for a positive way through the grief, although this was incredibly difficult in the early days.
However, I was helped by…

Projects – For us there was no question but that we must immediately launch a campaign for changes at Kingston riverside to make the area safer and to ensure that no-one else would have to endure the trauma that we lived through.

This was achieved over three years or so and helped enormously in giving me the feeling that I was 'doing something' in the light of our personal tragedy. James' legacy is that the area is now safer, brighter and altogether more appealing to the many visitors who pass along this stretch of the Thames. The council was receptive and helpful to us in our campaign and this in itself helped me to keep the impetus to ensure that changes were made."

I also discussed the extensive effect of losing a child, which takes a long time to realise:

"The ripple effect is much greater than at first anyone anticipates. The early days of grief mean that you close in on yourself, surround yourself with a numbing cloak simply to get through each second, each minute, and each hour. When you slowly begin to emerge from shock, blinking as if in sudden daylight, you realise that your social life, your family and friendships, your work/life balance are all irrevocably altered and damaged by what has happened.

You have to start all over again to rebuild the relationships that hitherto you took for granted. It is not uncommon to feel like a social leper in the early days because the majority of people simply do not know how to deal you or with the enormity of your loss. People also talk a lot about 'significant dates' and difficult days. In fact, beyond the obvious trials of the anniversary, birthday, Christmas etc, nearly every day can be significant in some way to a bereaved parent."

As I had been asked to elucidate on how counsellors can help bereaved parents, I also admonished them a little, telling them, "Don't say facile things to a bereaved parent, such as, 'I know how you feel. My granny died last week.'"

There is a WORLD of difference between someone who has lived her life into her seventies or eighties, and a 19-year-old on the cusp of adulthood. It is not helpful to tell us that you understand how we feel, whatever your loss, it will be different to ours.

Similarly, please don't say, 'At least he /she didn't suffer' or 'You are brave to cope with it the way you do.' No bereaved parent wants to be told he or she is brave. I am not brave. Strong, resourceful and resilient perhaps, but not brave!

Some people make the mistake of telling us to count our blessings because we still have our other children. Of course we are grateful if we have not lost our only child, but you must remember that we are grieving for the one who has gone, not the one(s) that we still have. It may be possible to count blessings and be grateful later along the line, but not in the early stages of grief.

I do not define myself by the loss of my son now, although I did so in the first couple of years, but I do reflect on my life in distinct terms of 'before' and 'after' he died. I suspect this is inevitable for anyone who has suffered sudden loss. There can be quite a blurring of the memories as time passes. I find myself now sometimes questioning whether James was here for this or that family event, because I can't remember whether it took place before or after he passed.

As a bereaved parent, you learn to make allowances for the fact that people don't know how to deal with you.

I read of a bereaved parent who hit the nail on the head when she said, 'I discovered there is a facial expression people save especially for bereaved parents, which I call "the look." It is one of heartbreaking concern and, whilst I am always touched, it is not particularly helpful. Eventually, it begins to grate. Grief does not make one patient.'

It is important for people to try to treat you as normally as possible, although this may be difficult, particularly with the recently bereaved.

I am no closer to perfect than the next person, and do not underestimate my grief path which has not been without spells of wrenching despair, tears and railing at the Fates for what has happened to us.

Thankfully, I have found that these very raw, acutely agonising moments do mellow with time."

People shy away from mentioning the child who has died for fear of upsetting the grieving parent. I pointed out that this is ridiculous, saying, "How could we be any more upset than we already are? If now I ask about my friends' sons and daughters, yes, I do really want to know! We are sometimes just too polite for our own good.

One of the greatest fears of the bereaved parent is that their child will be forgotten. As time passes, it is natural for the loss to recede in other people's minds. But every bereaved parent positively welcomes any opportunity to speak about their child so do not be afraid to say his or her name.

There is a quote by Elizabeth Edwards that illustrates this perfectly: 'If you know someone who has lost a child, and you're afraid to mention them because you think you might make them sad by reminding them that they died - you're not reminding them. They didn't forget they died. What you're reminding them of is that you remembered that they lived, and that is a great gift.'"

I also emphasised how important it is for the bereaved to spend time with others who really understand. I continue to meet and exchange emails with other bereaved parents, and this provides an invaluable mutual support network.

I further expressed to the group a premise that I feel I have learned over time, "It is my view that bereaved people deal with their loss in two distinct ways. There are those who can't or don't want to change, and those who *do* want to change and will do everything in their power to do this. You will not be surprised to hear that I place myself in the latter group.

I appreciate that in many ways I am lucky. James was not murdered, nor did he suffer a long illness, and although we have a modern day blended family it is not a fragmented family. Thus I have loving and compassionate support.

Despite that I still feel parental guilt – guilt that I could not prevent what happened to James, and guilt that my husband, daughter and stepchildren, and all those who knew James, have to go through their lives without his being here to share all that is to follow."

I wished to convey how grief changes with the passage of time, and said something along the lines of, "In the early days of grief it is impossible to find optimism and hope for the future, looking backward is far less painful in some respects than looking forward to a future without your child. There are many ways forward that gradually become 'do-able' in time.

For myself, I found it helpful to keep a journal, write for TCF and DSN and recently, for some light relief, to join a creative writing group that has allowed me to express emotions and enjoy sharing the response of a group of people who are not directly involved with my bereavement. Picking up on old hobbies is also a great help in restoring normality to a life, which ceases to feel normal. New normal ultimately becomes the order of the day.

But don't be deceived by our air of ordinariness, which is borne out of the donning of a carefully honed mask to disguise the pain we are still feeling, and will always feel to some degree.

The process of dealing with loss saps confidence to a huge extent, and I found that challenging myself with charity walks, going to the gym, taking up running all helped me to regain my self confidence. Learning complementary therapies – Reiki, holistic massage and reflexology helped to give me new directions to focus on and think about.

Ultimately I hope I convey the message that it is possible to achieve a kind of independence from your grief and choose if and when you wish to visit it.

Counselling has an invaluable though indefinable role to play in this. It is one more tool in the armoury against the potential meltdown of inescapable grief.

There are times I still need to sit quietly with my thoughts of James and visit anew the sense of loss but these are less frequent and less acutely painful."

I closed my talk, somewhat surprised to find that around 25 minutes had passed, by emphasising to the group, "People say to me when they hear of James' death, 'What a waste!' But I can tell you, that I do not consider a single moment of his life a waste. The waste lies in the lack of the future that he should have had, not the time he was with us.

With a level of absorption of my grief that has come with time, I can think of James' life as a complete short story, rather than an unfinished novel."

Afterwards, there was an opportunity for the counsellors to ask questions. Then they broke into smaller satellite groups and discussed all that they had heard. I went to each group in turn to answer their – sometimes quite searching – questions.

I am sure you will wonder how I felt at the end of the evening. Well, I realised how very empowering it is to 'hold' an audience, and I understood for the first time the attraction of being on a stage. Although I was emotionally drained afterwards, this was offset by a wonderful sense of achievement. I was proud of myself for having the courage to speak and proud that I was able to share my James with such a willing and empathic audience.

I was gratified to get complimentary feedback after the evening. In particular one of the counsellors took the trouble to write to me to say that my talk had altered the way she communicates with a close friend who lost her daughter, making her feel more comfortable with talking about her own offspring.

Such a response made me feel that I really achieved something worthwhile, whilst contributing to a better understanding of the issues of the grieving parent in relation to their counselling needs.

I can only talk about grief from the perspective of a mother's loss. The journalist Paul Clabburn, who in 2007 lost his 14-year-old son Tom when he died in his sleep from a rare heart condition, writes: [3]"The perception that men and women grieve differently – for example that a man might be more inclined to bottle it up while a woman is freer to express her emotions – may well be true.

However, that doesn't alter the fact that, in my experiences, whatever your gender, when your child is cut from your life you bleed and keep on bleeding. There's no 'right' way to deal with that except the way that's right for you. Finding that way, of course, is the problem."

He goes on to say, "I didn't consciously re-evaluate my life or my outlook. Life carries on with a Tom-shaped hole in its fabric. Sometimes it rips further, sometimes it's less frayed, but it's always there. It's there in a way I accept yet occasionally resent. Sometimes it makes me smile but more often it makes me sad, a sense of longing for whatever might have been."

I can relate to the fabric analogy that Paul uses in terms of grief. Early grief can feel like wearing a damp grey, clinging cloak of misery. Over time, the cloak settles into kinder folds, but it can never be removed. A tightness here, an unravelling there, will always remind me that I must pay homage to my grief at times. The difference now is that I can choose when to pull up the hood of my invisible garment, wrap myself in its darkness, and revisit the very core of my loss with control and at a time of my own choosing.

[3] First published in *The Independent*, 9 July 2013

It is true to say that there is no manual or text book that adequately describes, for a bereaved parent or for those counselling a bereaved parent, how to deal with the bereavement. We do not automatically know how to behave, how to grieve, how to make sense of the turmoil of emotions that comes with this particular form of loss. I believe it is vital to keep examining, exploring, researching and reviewing the reactive process of working through loss so as to offer the best possible options for counselling and supporting those who have suffered unexpected and untimely loss.

As a photographer, I have always been a recorder of events. My father encouraged me from an early age. He used to say, "Photographs capture a moment and freeze it in time. They are precious."

And I followed his cue, diligently recording with my camera birthdays, celebrations, family events and so on. Our family are great readers too. My mother always kept a diary, a habit I have followed from time to time, and we all enjoyed writing. When my parents moved to Cornwall, we often exchanged short letters just to keep in touch. It is a great pity that my parents died before the internet really got going for I am sure that my dad in particular would have been a keen silver surfer.

Thus, it came as no surprise to me that I find comfort in writing about James. My early scribing, in a daily journal was full of despair and heartfelt misery and was definitely not fit to share. In fact, I ceremoniously shredded my journal from the first year of loss because I felt it had nothing to bring to anyone for the future. But as time passed, I realised that writing about loss is a great healer. Writing heals your heart page by page.

There is comfort in documenting your progress along the grief journey, especially when you can look back and see the gradual lightening of the dark days of early loss.

Writing solely for myself is one thing. But writing for an audience is quite another. I have written a piece each year around the time of the anniversary of James' passing and disseminated this writing to a selected audience – family and friends and more widely to TCF and DSN. It is heart-warming when I receive feedback from people who say that my writing helps them. I never really saw the gift in being able to express myself in the written word before, but now I understand that I am an expert in grief and I can share some of that expertise in areas where it is appreciated. That is a satisfying feeling.

Writing achieves something very special in allowing us to remember. By recording memories from across the years, you are holding close the essence of your child. Not only that but you are informing other people of those particular nuances that went to make up his or her personality, and eventually people who never met your child can nonetheless visualise the person they were.

At James' funeral service, the minister, David Hampshire, said of James, "In the coming days let us continue to tell his story, at times it will make us laugh and at others cry – both are right."

And I have continued to tell his story, which is the very cornerstone and foundation of my own grief path. Telling the stories of James' life and how our lives have continued since his death weaves the threads of memory that bind us to him.

James enriched my life and the lives of many others; his death gave me the greatest test of my own lifetime and gave me an acute awareness of the fragility of all our lives. The major hurdle of accepting the sudden loss of a child (and I argue that you cannot ever truly accept it) is made an easier challenge if you try to reason it out through writing and expressing the gamut of emotions that you experience as you traverse the bumpy fields of grief.

In the immediate aftermath of sudden loss, my mind was full of questions. "How could I survive this? What would happen to our family? How on earth could I ever console my husband/daughter/stepfamily?"

Writing did not give me the answers, but it helped to take the raw edge off the agony as I considered the best way to tackle a way forward. At the beginning I wrote lists and ticked things off as I achieved them – small milestones often, but the satisfaction of seeing a list of checked items spurred me on. Grief is also a great cause of amnesia I still find that I need to write things down in order to remember to do them. If I do not, I will promptly forget them.

Eventually, writing and reading began to help me to accept the reality of what had happened. Through reading other accounts of healing after loss and adapting the advice contained in them to suit my own circumstances, gradually I came to understand the power of words to comfort, sustain and inform me in moving along my own path.

One of the greatest questions that torments the newly bereaved is of course "Why?" And this is something that I suspect is never satisfactorily answered for most people. But with the distance that time affords me in my grief, I can now believe that knowing 'why' would not add anything to my general state of being today.

81

Writing affords a degree of control over grief. Expressing emotions is cathartic, whether they are positive or negative. Writing provides me with the means to communicate with James. I can write a letter to him; write a poem for him or write a card to place at his grave. There is satisfaction in all these.

It does not matter if you think you cannot write. Even single words on a page can evoke memories and emotions, and the beauty of writing is that you do not need to share it unless you so choose.

Writing out my grief has been an important part of my healing. There came a point however where I wished to write creatively in a different direction and I joined a local Adult Education Creative Writing Group.

This was a very enriching and useful experience. The group focused mainly on the mechanics of writing fiction although some class members were working on autobiographical pieces. Certainly attending the group helped me to hone my skills in being self expression. I learned too how to use dialogue in writing to make it more interesting and how to incorporate other voices into my writing.

I learned that writing is a skill like any other that needs practice and it was a great confidence booster to read out a piece of work and have it gently critiqued by other members of the group. It was also fascinating to listen to other people's work and to learn how they approach their writing. I enjoyed being set homework tasks and they certainly concentrated the creative mind For example we might be given an opening sentence such as 'The door swung slowly open' and have to then write 6-700 words in the form of a short story. These exercises were challenging but enjoyable and the opportunity to write what I term 'light and fluffy' pieces, offsets the sometimes difficult task of expressing darker emotions. I was lucky that my tutor was a good class leader and the other members of the class were interesting and compassionate individuals. The writing group was a safe forum in which to share some of my lighter pieces although I shied away from telling too much of my story. It was neither the right time nor the right place and in fact the writing group became a place for light relief and the release of stress through sharing words.

For anyone considering writing as a tool to express or relieve their grief I would say it is worth giving it a try. You can start with a blank piece of paper or a computer screen and write a single word. Sit back and wait and it is almost inevitable that the creative juices will start to flow. If you practise this regularly you will find as I have that it becomes easier to find a writing voice to tell your own individual story.

I learned a great deal at writing group but ultimately realised that I am not cut out to write a novel – at least until I have told James' story and the story of our grief path.

Writing remains a significant tool in the armoury against my loss and I will never tire of telling James' story to anyone who wishes to listen. This too is part of his legacy.

Finding You

Where are you now, my lovely son?
I hear your voice in the sigh of the wind
I see your smile in the brightness of the sun
I know your growth in the shifting seasons
Where are you now, my dear lad?
I taste the salt of your tears for our loss4
I feel your charisma in the velvet darkness
And your laughter echoes in my mind
Where are you now, my handsome youngster?
You were the arrow to my bow
You shot into my life, and raced ahead
Impatient to live as much as you might
Where are you now, my beautiful boy?
You brought such vibrancy and joy
Your life too short, but so well lived
You bequeathed us many stories
Where are you now, my strong young man?
You build my strength in this different life
Your footsteps follow in my shadow
And your presence aids my courage
Where are you now, my sweet child?
I feel your soul beating on in my heart
I will always hear you when you call
Death does not separate, after all.

Andrea Corrie, 2007

84

Chapter 5

Butterflies, Rainbows and a Toolbox

Come to the edge, he said
We are afraid, they said
Come to the edge, he said
They came to the edge
He pushed them and they flew
Come to the edge, Life said
They said: We are afraid
Come to the edge, Life said
They came. It pushed them...
And they flew

Guilliame Apollinaire French Poet

It strikes me that after bereavement, when we are searching for different routes to emotional support, it is a common response to turn to spiritual beliefs.

One day, about a year after James died, Stella phoned me and she sounded brighter than she had since his death.
"I have had a really good weekend, mum," she said.
"I have been on a Reiki healing course and I found it very helpful. I think you might, too."

We went on to talk about Reiki, what it is, how it works and so on and I felt optimistic that it could help me to mentally process the trauma of grieving.

I don't subscribe to a formal religious doctrine as such and my faith is a somewhat shaky affair so I felt uplifted by the thought that there could be something out there to help me.

Many people have no idea what Reiki is (I didn't either) but when I looked on the internet I found it described as, "a form of healing utilising the laying on of hands in order to heal people with physical, emotional, mental or spiritual problems."

Reiki treatments draw upon energies and direct these to the energy body of a client in order to stimulate their immune system and the body's own repair systems. Reiki cannot be learned from a book. The techniques are learned by use of the energy itself. In order to start this process a Reiki student needs to be introduced to the energy by a suitably qualified and experienced Reiki master/teacher within a Reiki class. Reiki is taught at three levels; healer (for self first and foremost, family and friends), practitioner (for use with the general public) and master/teacher (for further spiritual advancement, empowerment and the ability to teach and attune others).

I was intrigued enough to seek out a Reiki teacher and found one locally. I signed up for a course in Reiki I, the first level, and the classes were uplifting, enjoyable and helpful. Once I had learned the technique of self-healing using Reiki, I was able to use it to good effect. One of the greatest benefits I have found through learning Reiki has been the ability to meditate and to sit quietly with my grief.

At the first level of Reiki, I found that self-care had entered my existence in a new way. Part of the commitment at Level 1 is to practise a full session of Reiki self-treatment for 21 days in order to form a daily habit that for many, myself included, then becomes a habit for life. I felt immediately more relaxed when I got into this daily routine and started sleeping better. Writing at this time also helped release my grief and I feel sure my daily Reiki practice was supporting me in this.

I learned to shield, protect and ground my own energies before I started any task that might challenge me. I found it particularly helpful to use Reiki at night before I fell asleep. Visualising positive protection for all my loved ones and myself was uplifting and useful. The feeling that Reiki brings of becoming centred and balanced in the present is a boon. The gentle, therapeutic nature of Reiki allowed me to accept the reality of my loss in a way that aided me in moving forward in the healing process.

I went on to learn Reiki Level II and practised on family and friends and a few clients, finding that once I had mastered the techniques of channelling Reiki energy, I was able to detach sufficiently from my own problems to be an effective therapist. This brought me a great deal of satisfaction. It is true to say that one cannot offer healing without attaining a level of healing of one's self and being able to practise Reiki on others underlined my own healing progress.

Finally, I attended a two day (third level) Reiki Master course in the beautiful surroundings of Chalice Well Gardens in Glastonbury, Somerset, which enabled me to focus on this lovely therapy at a higher level.

Regular spiritual practice, prayer or introspective meditation can be beneficial in establishing comforting rituals and routines which are helpful in processing sorrow and grief in manageable small 'bites'. Certainly I find that when I practise Reiki daily, building it into my morning preparations before work, even if I am spending only five or ten minutes, I feel somehow more balanced and even in mood overall. There are no rules for practising self-healing.

While I would recommend Reiki as a good way of helping to process grief, others may be drawn to other forms of healing such as spiritual healing. All healing modalities appear to share a common purpose to heal gently and compassionately.

They do not replace conventional medicine, if for example you have a diagnosed organic illness or disease, but I have found those that I have explored to be helpful adjuncts in the process of emotional healing. The term 'complementary' means just that – complementary therapies are there to support and enhance other prescribed treatments that may be offered by the health services.

My Reiki teacher encourages her students to keep a positive outlook on life and focus on trying as far as possible to avoid negativity. For example, she says, "Don't watch films or television programmes which depress or upset you. If you are distressed by the evening news, simply turn it off that day and don't feel guilty about that."

At first, I found this view be rather blinkered but it taught me the important lesson that we retain the choice of how we wish to feel and we make those decisions almost unconsciously many times each day. If I am feeling a bit low or fragile I avoid reading the daily paper or watching the news. If, however, I am feeling strong and brave, I will do both. It is a good balance to find.

If you do not have a religious faith that draws you to formalised services, this does not preclude you from following a spiritual path to help you find a better understanding of your loss and how you can process it.

You do not necessarily need to learn a healing modality, but for most people it is probably helpful to have the structure of some teaching to lay down the basics. Even the most basic meditation is a controlled brain exercise that links in with your breathing and allows you to sit for a short time in real stillness, without the day to day clamour that inevitably surrounds us.

Meditation can be as simple as sitting with your eyes closed and breathing comfortably. It can be useful to set a timer for a short spell at first, as it requires discipline to take time out for a session of meditation, but even ten minutes on a daily basis is useful. If you are open to whatever comes into your mind as you meditate, it becomes a relaxed and comfortable way to explore the innermost thoughts and emotions that swirl around in your mind.

If you have never meditated or used visualisation techniques before, the following is a simple symbolic guided meditation that you may find useful.

The rainbow is an ancient symbol of hope and eternal life. The colours of the rainbow are pure and clear and in spiritual terms, each has a different energy attributed to it.

During some quiet time close your eyes and visualise a rainbow in a blue sky. While visualising the rainbow, imagine in your mind all the qualities that you loved in the person who died. Call to mind special memories of the person. Whatever they may be, take each one of those qualities and memories and place them in the bands of the rainbow you are seeing in your mind's eye.

You can take as little or as long a time as you need. When you feel ready and with your eyes still closed, reach up with your mind or physically and one by one, pull down the colours of the rainbow, starting with the outer band of red, then orange, yellow, green, blue, indigo and violet. Imagine you have pulled all the coloured bands around yourself like a protective cloak of many colours.

If you feel drawn to expand the meditation to others, then visualise your friends and family, neighbours and colleagues similarly cloaked in your rainbow.

After you have sat with your rainbow for as long as you wish, take a few deep breaths, wriggle your fingers and toes to ground yourself back into reality, recreate the room in your mind and open your eyes.

The rainbow you have created is individual to you because it contains only your memories. You can call upon it for comfort at any time.

I consider that within the environment of meditation, through placing yourself in that special individual place that is yours and yours alone, the body relaxes and calms and this enables healing to take place.

It seems to me that all spiritual teaching encourages us to live with strength and positivity, not weakness and negativity.

Having learnt Reiki, I became interested in the integration of mind, body and spirit in holistic therapies and in 2007 I signed up for a holistic massage therapist course.

Before you can practise as a massage therapist, it is necessary to complete an in-depth anatomy and physiology course and there are both practical and written examinations at the end of the year. The prospect was daunting but I found it exciting to be learning new skills.

As a species, we seriously underestimate the power of touch, particularly in relation to comforting people and making them feel better. Thus I enjoyed learning how to give a relaxing and de-stressing massage. It was satisfying to get good feedback from my massage clients, particularly when I was learning and practising on willing friends and family who were happy to volunteer for case studies.

After passing my exams, in terms of complementary therapies, I now had two strings to my bow – the energy therapy Reiki and the body system of massage. I wanted to go on to explore another modality and the following year I discovered reflexology, which is a magical treatment – far more than a foot massage – that neatly fulfilled my desire to find a treatment that really unites body, mind, and spirit. The principle of reflexology is that certain areas of the feet correspond to the body's systems – neurological, digestive, skeletal etc., and by stimulating the reflexes blood flow is increased to these areas allowing for healing, stimulating or soothing as appropriate.

A reflexology treatment brings about a state of deep relaxation. The therapy seems to aid the body's own healing processes, which may help return it to its natural stage of balance and wellbeing. I would say too, that reflexology can benefit those who feel numb with grief. The non-invasive and safe nature of the therapy encourages people to feel nurtured and balanced with clearer thinking.

Somehow, reflexology combines the physical advantages of massage, such as increased circulation and a soothing touch with the more spiritual aspects of channelling energy through the practitioner to the recipient. It is hard to describe the quality of its spiritual side. Energy can take so many forms as this definition suggests: "Sharp as a hook, fine as a hair, taut as a musical string, dead as a rock, smooth as a flowing stream, or as continuous as a string of pearls." (Taken from the preface to Jan Williamson's book "Precision Reflexology" and unattributed).

Reflexology is a lovely treatment to give. It is physically easier than performing massage and it is amazing how much a therapist can pick up from someone's feet. I have found that during reflexology treatments, I am also giving Reiki (with the client's permission of course) and a degree of foot massage. Reflexology treatment alone combines all the skills that I have learned.

Through learning these various therapies I found that I increased my self-confidence and understood myself better and I am sure that they all help with my ability to process my grief.

I am a bit of a dabbler when it comes to trying New Age things, and I have also touched on crystal healing. I have several sets of oracle and angel cards. Sometimes I like to pick a card during my morning meditation that will give me a message for the day – it is a nice focus that provides a distraction from the mundane tasks that face us all on a daily basis.

A whole new source of reading material also opens itself up to you if you become involved in spiritual and energy matters.

I particularly enjoyed Diana Cooper's *A Little Light on the Spiritual Laws* and anything written by Paulo Coelho, to name just a couple of examples. Paulo Coelho, most famous perhaps for his book *The Alchemist* writes wonderfully uplifting and optimistic thoughts. A new vocabulary of positive words such as 'intention', 'affirmation' and 'manifestation' has found its way into my mind's dictionary.

Essential oils and essences, perfumed candles and incense sticks can all alter the feel and energy in a room and provide comfort when meditating, sitting listening to music or simply having a think!

It is interesting to consider what induces us to follow a spiritual path following the devastating loss of our children. My friend Linda talked to me about how she has changed spiritually since the loss of her son Tom. In fact, she and I have followed similar paths and she echoes my own discoveries in spirituality, although the modalities we follow are not quite the same.

She says: "It's the initial devastation, when you are cut to the core. When the loss happens, you undergo some form of transformation right to your heart and soul. There is a paradigm shift, a definite change in your being.

Really, I suppose spiritual things started to find me rather than the other way round. Very soon after Tom's death, I heard from Catherine, a girl whom Tom met in Australia. They had obviously hit it off, because he was trying to change his flights to go back to spend more time with her.

Catherine wrote: 'It was a growly day on the beach. I sat down and began to write Tom a letter about my feelings and how much I missed him. The clouds were gathering and it was windy, the sea was rough and grey. Suddenly, as I finished writing, the clouds rolled away, the sun came out and there was an amazing rainbow right across the bay. I felt sure it was sent to me from Tom.'"

After that, Linda tells how there was a memorial service at Gordon's, Tom's school, followed by a rugby match between the school and Tom's rugby club, Weybridge Vandals. As the game drew to a close, a rainbow appeared right between the goal posts even though it was a dry and bright day.

Linda's experiences of rainbows echo ours with butterflies. These spiritual symbols are a great comfort, especially in the early days of grief, when we are desperate for any links we can find with our children. We really do need to know that they are all right in the realms of spirit. The song *Build me up, Buttercup* reminds us of James, and pops up in the most unlikely places (most notably Thailand!), while Linda has a similar link with the song *Somewhere over the Rainbow* which was randomly played when she recently arrived on holiday in Portugal, in a tiny restaurant in a quiet and remote fishing village.

Linda described her spiritual journey, "I got into spiritual healing through my friend Ann. She was ill with breast cancer and asked me to go with her to Harry Edwards Healing Sanctuary at Shere, where I had healing too. I realised this was my path and it was important for me to follow it.

I felt as though this was something Tom was telling me to do and I did not question it. In fact, I have almost completed my two-year healer course now.

I have also had readings that validate my healing beliefs and I am quite convinced that this is part of Tom's legacy to me, to offer healing to others whilst at the same time healing myself."

I met some of the Harry Edwards˙ healers at a Mind, Body, Spirit event and as a result, I visited Harry Edwards Healing Sanctuary on an open day to have some healing.

As I was walking around enjoying the atmosphere at HEHS, who should I bump into but Linda! She was with her friend Geraldine who, it turned out, worked at the primary school where James did his work experience. This lady was able to tell me what she remembered of James, and it was wonderful; it was just like having a little visit from him. This was particularly special given the timing; it was the day before Mother's Day!

Linda's view, which accords entirely with mine, is that, "Getting into healing, whatever modality it may be, restores some of the confidence of the person you were before. Healing becomes a way of life that requires a lot of honesty and because of the experience we have had, we are more compassionate and empathetic. We are able to use our traumatic experiences and turn them into something positive."

It matters not whether you study Reiki, spiritual healing, or if you embrace formal religious beliefs. As Linda so rightly says, "We are all climbing the same mountain," so the path we take to the summit is immaterial; it is really a matter of choosing - or being guided to - whatever suits each individual.

Some events are spiritual in an unexpected way, and one such event which stays in my mind is when I went paragliding in Turkey. This was either a very brave or a very foolish thing to do, depending on your point of view.

We were driven up an extremely steep road complete with sheer drop hairpin bends, until we finally reached the top of the rocky hills some 6,500 feet above the tourist resort of Olu Deniz. We had been watching the colourful canopies of the gliders coming down over the beach for a few days now, and I had already made up my mind that I just had to try this daredevil event.

In fact, this is a good example of the recklessness which can sometimes come after deep trauma and grief. I believe that a fundamental change in thinking occurs; I definitely feel these days that life is too short not to have a go at things I would not previously have considered.

As Stella often says, "Mum, you rarely regret the things you have a go at, but it is easy to regret the things you don't try."

Such positivity was missing from my psyche in the few minutes that I stood in blazing heat being zipped into a flying suit, but it was too late to turn back now.

I was safely harnessed to a young Turkish paragliding pilot who had assured me he was very experienced and would look after me, and almost before I knew it, we had taken a few short stumbling steps to the edge and we were aloft. I can hardly describe the exhilaration of this, the closest I will ever get to flying. If this is what being in spirit is like, feeling weightless and ageless, then bring it on! I laughed out loud with sheer delight, amazed by the wonderful feeling of freedom I was experiencing.

"This one's for you, James!" I found myself saying out loud as we looped and twirled above the azure sea. Up in the sky, the quiet was profound. Apart from the sound of the breeze rustling the canopy, there was a marvellous, peaceful, comfortable silence. I was not afraid as I placed all my trust, and indeed my life, in the skilled hands of my paraglider pilot who seemed amused at my enthusiasm. Once we were back on terra firma, I continued to feel as though I had been spiritually uplifted and closer to James than I had been since his passing. Somehow I felt that he knew that I had done it and had been with me as we swooped through the sky.

In fact I enjoyed my paragliding experience so much, I repeated it before the end of our holiday.

In everyday life, our decision making process is easy. We start from the moment we open our eyes ... What shall I wear to work today? What shall I eat for breakfast? Shall I go to the supermarket before the office, or after? My mind has probably answered ten such questions for me before I put on my dressing gown.

But when a child is lost you are expected, in the midst of the chaotic maelstrom of your grief, to make a series of important decisions, quickly and efficiently. It is quite absurd but equally a tribute to our mental faculties that we find ourselves able to observe the traditions and requirements following a death as well as plan a funeral.

One such decision was for us to settle on where we would have James' ashes scattered. His father's remains had been placed in a certain part of the gardens at Woking Crematorium. After a great deal of discussion, Shaun, Stella and I agreed that this was where James' ashes should be, too. We agreed on the siting of a memorial plaque and a planting of a yellow rosebush. The wording of this plaque is an absolute testament to the generous heart and spirit of Shaun, for he agreed, in fact he suggested, that James' father should be acknowledged on this plaque too. The final wording on which we agreed sat well with all of us.

The arrangement in place at the crematorium is that if you so wish, you can witness your loved one's ashes being strewn in a ceremonial way, with prayers and/or a blessing. However, having gone through the agonies of one funeral service, we decided against putting ourselves through a further ceremony. Thus we agreed that James' remains would be scattered around the sundial in the Shakespeare garden on a given date in October. I was told that this would be done early in the morning before the start of any funeral services that day.

On the appointed day, I drove to the crematorium before I went to work, judging my timing carefully. I was able to see, by the circle of ashes in the grass, that the deed had been done.

I did not feel squeamish or upset by the sight, rather it was comforting to have visible proof that the ceremony had been performed as it should have been. No-one was around but it made me feel very close to James to know that this thing had been quietly and respectfully carried out.

We did not need to be there.

Some parents need to visit the crematorium or graveyard regularly. I do not. I get a better sense of James' presence when we go to Kingston, but just occasionally I feel the need to visit the crematorium and lay some flowers by his plaque, usually around his birthday or the anniversary date. It has to be remembered that what suits one person does not suit another and no-one is wrong, or right, in this regard. I follow my heart, my thoughts, my spirit and my soul in deciding when and what observances to make for my son. I believe too that these moments are guided for me through spirit.

There are many different signs and messages from spirit to consider if you are a believer. Certainly at first, it is hard not to see signs of your lost one at every turn. For us, butterflies symbolise James. We had so many sightings of them in the early months after his passing, in odd places and at unusual times. The butterfly is a common spiritual symbol for life after death because of its metamorphosis, or transformation, from a caterpillar that crawls on the ground to an ethereal creature that flies through the air. It is also symbolic of personal growth and spiritual rebirth.

Shaun and I visited the crematorium to see James' memorial plaque once it was in place. The day was overcast and drizzly. We were standing in the garden looking at the plaque when a large butterfly landed on the nearby sundial (where James' ashes had previously been

99

strewn). The butterfly flew up and brushed my head, before circling Shaun and flying along a path. We were just exclaiming over it when it suddenly returned and landed on the left side of my chest, just above the top of my T-shirt, remaining there for at least 20 seconds, before flying away. We both felt tremendously uplifted by the presence of the butterfly and felt most strongly that it was a sign from James.

I have consulted psychic mediums and had various readings over the years.

I believe in an afterlife, but it is sometimes difficult to see things as hard evidence that James is sending messages. It seems that he is more likely to make his presence felt to others than to me – most notably my friend Pauline. And she has had many experiences which point to his being around.

A few weeks after we lost James, I asked Pauline to pass on his details to a friend of hers, who is a medium. I felt very strongly that I couldn't 'place' James, and I needed some reassurance about this. Pauline gave the medium a photograph of James and told her only that he died in an accident. The medium and two colleagues met together and focused on James.

The feedback I received from Pauline was greatly comforting to me. The medium said she saw him stretching up his arms and simply losing his balance and falling into the river, without distress.

However, what really comforted me was the wording that was used. As a child, if James ever did anything wrong, whether deliberately or by accident, he would say, "I didn't mean to do it." This was the exact wording that came through to the medium and the other two people with her.

I had a reading from a medium in 2010 which proved to be uncannily accurate, not just for the things she said about James but about our house move in 2012.

At the time I saw her, we were pondering where to live but at that point had not decided where we would go. Briefly, I had a wish to live by the sea – we made some new friends who live in Sussex and we were attracted to the area, but in the end it was not a practicable plan. However it was under consideration at the time.

The medium said to me, "You are thinking about a move. You are thinking about living by water ... But this isn't going to happen the way you are expecting it to."

At the time, I thought no more of it. However in 2012 I discovered whilst out for my first run after our move to our new home that we are only five minutes away from the towpath of the local canal. We did not realise it was so close before we moved.

Since we came to live here, I have grown to love the area and I find being in the tree-lined and peaceful environment as I run along the canal path very healing and uplifting indeed. I do wonder if that was what the medium meant during the reading.

As well as a feeling that James has an awareness of our lives continuing without his presence here with us, I often sense my mother close to me and I am certain she shares her strength and wisdom with me mentally, particularly at difficult times. She has been mentioned several times by mediums as being at my side or just at my shoulder. I find this comforting and not in the least surprising as we were very close.

There is always such a longing for 'just one more' conversation with our child. But sadly, it cannot be. Writing letters is one way around this and I have done it several times. But the irrefutable finality of the loss of the physical presence of the person and their ability to respond in conversation is extremely frustrating to say the least. Sometimes I get inspiration to write poetry, and the poems I have written since James died feel as though they have come from him as well as myself.

I often feel him near me, I often hear his voice quite clearly in my mind, and at these times I have goose pimples or feel cold, as though I have been gently brushed by his spirit. These incidents are of great comfort.

Extreme trauma leads to many questions and I think that our desire for answers often draws us along a spiritual path that we would not formerly have considered or approached. As Stephanie Ericsson wrote in *Companion Through the Darkness:* "Grief is the time when we are blessed with the opportunity to complete a natural process of spiritual death and rebirth before our own death."

If the loss can be viewed as a catalyst to explore a spiritual path, in certain respects I feel both stronger and wiser for the deep level of shock I have undergone and the fact that I have been able to break through the negativity of it to emerge phoenix like, stronger and with a shift in my own belief system. I have seen such a paradigm described as a specific way of thinking, seeing and experiencing our reality; a lens through which we perceive and frame our world. If that is so, then I would say I have a far broader sense of not just what is around me, but what has gone before and what is still to come in future existences.

In common with many others, I find comfort in the ritual of lighting candles. The simple act of placing a lighted candle in the room, particularly at dusk or on a gloomy day, is very meaningful. The flame of the candle provides a meditative focus. The symbolism of light into darkness throughout the ages and across the world is uplifting.

Every year, TCF holds an international candle-lighting ceremony and at 7.00pm in whatever time zone, candles are lit for our lost children. It is a powerful and heart-warming ritual with an international sense of ceremony.

Rituals affirm landmarks in our lives – birthdays, anniversaries, weddings, baptisms, etc.

Whenever I go into a church I habitually light three candles. One is for James, one is for my late parents and the third is for everyone else. I like to cover all bases!
In the early days of grief it is practically impossible to find any light in the darkness. But the symbolic act of lighting a candle and mentally sending light to yourself, your family and friends and your lost child is helpful in many ways.

Some people may prefer to pray, rather than meditate. What we are doing when we pray for help is turning our problems over to the Divine.

As part of the healing process, having a place to take the feelings and share them helps us to not always have to hold onto them, especially when they become too overpowering.

The act of 'giving our grief to a higher realm' can be a powerful release for many. Some feel that prayer is one of the greatest acts of charity that can be given for those who have died and no-one can fail to be moved when witnessing large scale demonstrations of prayer on television, on significant war anniversaries, for example. Anything that helps observation of the rhythms of life and death in the natural world can help in processing and normalising the grief route.

Negativity in our grief thought processes is unhelpful – though it is something else that has to be worked through in the early days of loss. There is a term 'tragedy consciousness' where other people will say to you things like, "Oh how terrible. You must be devastated."

Of course we can understand people's need to try to sympathise and empathise with the tragedy that has happened, but over time I have come to realise that James' life was not incomplete – for him it ended at the time it was meant to, however hurtful and sad that was for those of us left here to continue living without him. Yes, his death is a waste of the years he can no longer live, but his life is most definitely not a waste to me, or to anyone else who knew him.

Hard though it is to see at the beginning, I think the acceptance of the difficulties of the grieving process ultimately leads to a level of wisdom not previously experienced. We all have inner strength to draw upon; the key is to recognise how to tap into it.

Spiritual practice has had the effect of giving me a greater awareness of my sense of self.

One of the key things that I have learned through studying complementary therapies is that we all deserve to reward ourselves and be kind to ourselves. It is very easy to be constantly looking after and being care-givers for other people – we are particularly used to that as parents – but there is definitely a time to take stock and look after our selves holistically – that is to say, looking after all our elements: mind, body and spirit.

The wholly affirmative aspect of spiritual practice may bring about positive change, personal empowerment and insight within the process of grieving. Certainly, I have found and continue to find this the case with a quest for exploration of many complementary healing modalities.

After James died, I found it very difficult to know what to do with his things. It has been a very gradual process, a slow but sure letting go, as bit by bit I have parted with his personal belongings. This is another entirely individual aspect of grief and I can only speak for my own way of dealing with it, whilst I have an awareness that others who prefer not to discard any of their children's possessions and keep their rooms just the way they were left.

Early on, I read online of memory boxes which people use to store precious mementoes, but I couldn't find quite the right thing. So, initially I bought three sturdy cardboard storage boxes that have an attractive Italianate cherub design. In these I placed various personal items such as James' diaries, some photo albums and special letters/cards.

One box is filled with his uni course work, which in fact I have never been able to look at. Handwriting is such an intensely personal thing and it still gives me a real jolt if I see James' writing.

One day about a year or so ago, I said to Shaun, "I've got a fancy to consolidate these cherub boxes into one place. I quite like the idea of a sturdy wooden blanket box that will accommodate all the bits and pieces."
Although I looked again on the internet and in various shops, I couldn't find anything that appealed.

But a few weeks later, Shaun arrived home from his work at BT (British Telecom) with an air of suppressed excitement.

"I've got something in the car," he said. "I really don't know if it's going to be right, but don't dismiss it at first glance."

By now of course I was intrigued, to say the least.

He led me out to the car and there reposed a large, solid, wooden BT toolbox with a hinged lid, painted a vivid canary yellow. It was so heavy it took both of us to lug it indoors.

It transpired that on a visit to BT stores, Shaun had been offered the box, which would otherwise have been scrapped. The boxes dated from circa 1980 and each BT van had been supplied with an onboard toolbox, the livery at that time being yellow.

Over a period of weeks Shaun performed a real labour of love, painstakingly stripping back the layers of yellow paint to reveal the attractively grained wood beneath.

Eventually, the box was varnished and the metal hinges were painted a glossy black, along with the hasp. The box is an individual and most precious item to store James' things, as well as being an attractive piece of furniture in its own right. It now stands in our lounge with a table lamp on top.

Some people favour memory quilts or soft toys made from their children's clothing. Again, I had seen various versions online but not been drawn to any one in particular. However, I was introduced via social media to the work of Lisa DeSouza who makes wonderfully individual keepsake bears and soft toys. She started off by designing fabric bears stitched from junior school uniforms or baby clothes, supplied by people who wanted keepsakes as their children grew older.

It so happened that some of James' clothes that I had stored in a cupboard became damp because of a leak from a heating pipe and distressingly, most of the shirts and T-shirts were spoiled by water damage. I kept just three shirts that were special; one he often wore on nights out, another he was wearing in the last photo I took of him in Brighton and finally, I had the shirt he wore to our wedding, just six weeks before his death.

I approached Lisa and she dealt with this first 'in memoriam' bear with sensitivity and warmth. Her exceptional skill resulted in a precious keepsake. Somehow our 'Jimbo bear' seems to possess a mischievous quality typical of James, and I am happy that I put the last of James' shirts to good use in this way.

There was sufficient material left to make a second bear for Stella and even though the fabric used is the same, the bears are quite individual in expression. Stella said she enjoyed having a tangible reminder of her little brother.

I think that as the grieving process moves forward, it becomes ever more important to preserve the memories of our lost children in whatever ways fulfil our needs. In holistic terms, my mind is nourished by spiritual practice.

My body responds to increased energy levels and endorphins through exercise. And finally my spirit is sustained by the comfort of James' presence round me, be it through signs from spirit or the physical statement of photographs and our memory bear.

Jimbo bear 2013

The Conversation

I spoke to heaven the other day,
I asked, "Do you think you could find a way,
To let me see him one more time,
Instead of talking to him through rhyme?
It's all very well to leave him flowers,
But I'd rather be speaking with him for hours
Curled up perhaps, in a comfy chair,
Ready to chat and some gossip share."
For quite a while no answer came,
And so despondent I became,
I sat right down and wrote him a letter,
And you know what? I felt much better.
I guess I manage without him here,
Because in my mind he is close and dear,
I have my memories to sustain,
Although that doesn't mean I won't complain.
I reckon there is Facebook in heaven,
And his friends must number a thousand and seven,
He can look down and watch over us all,
Whilst up there he is having such a ball.
He would hate to miss a single thing,
Be it a family birthday or a sign of spring,
I'm sure he must be pleased we carry on,
Living with meaning, even though he has gone.
Suddenly a sign came, it sounds absurd
But the visit from a little bird,
Singing in the garden trees,
Helped my sadness to release.
As time rolls by and my memories soften,
I think of my son at least as often,
And I remember him with much joy,
He is always close by, my sunny boy.

Andrea Corrie, Spring 2013

Chapter 6

And How Was Your Weekend?

Please ...
Talk About HIM
Talk about his lovely smile (What a Smile!!)
Share your memories of him
Share your sadness that he has gone
Ask what I loved about him
Tell me what you loved about him
Tell me what he brought to your life
Tell me you will miss him.
Say that he was beautiful
say that you loved him
But please don`t tell me "There is nothing I can say."

[Adapted from a poem by Becky Garrod]

The ripple effect of losing a child is inestimable. For my daughter Stella, James' sister, the loss has been devastating. It is a testament to her strength of character that two years after we lost James, she was able to put into words how she felt, for the purposes of this book. Stella had already had to face the loss of her father and grandparents.

Stella said, "I will never forget coming downstairs that warm, sunny Saturday morning to find a voicemail on my phone, from mum, saying to call her at work as soon as I got the message...I knew something was wrong from the tone of her voice and thought that she was going to tell me that our elderly dog, Jessica, had died...but the truth was to be much more shocking.

She told me very calmly that James had been missing since Wednesday night, that he had been on a night out with friends in Kingston and that he had left early and his friends all thought he had either gone home or was with other friends. Mum had started to worry when on the Thursday night he still wasn't home and Shaun had been to the police station to report him missing on the Friday. Mum had gone in to work on the Saturday (in retrospect, somehow knowing that she wouldn't be going in the following Monday). I asked mum where James had last been seen and as soon as she said the name of a particular nightclub I had a horrible, sinking pain in the pit of my stomach, as I knew that this club was on the riverbank of the Thames. Mum and I unconvincingly reassured each other that he was probably at someone's house or had maybe gone away on a whim, but even then I think we knew.

I carried on that Saturday as normally as possible. I remember telling my friends that he was missing and no-one really acknowledged the worry in my words. I went out that night with Pete, whom I had only been seeing for a couple of weeks, and we went to the Koola bar in Newquay. My irrational mind was playing tricks on me. I kept 'seeing' James on the dance floor below us and kept trying to believe that he was just being selfish and would suddenly bounce back through the door the next day.

Sadly it wasn't to be. I woke the next morning to my phone ringing and when I answered mum came on the phone saying, "Stella, it's the worst news." Then she couldn't say anymore and a police officer came on the phone saying how sorry he was but that they had recovered James' body from the Thames earlier that morning. Shaun took the phone from him and just kept saying "Oh Stella" and crying and I knew that our lives were about to change forever.

112

I put the phone down in a daze and burst into tears on Pete who just held me in disbelief. Then I went into my friend Elle's room and told her and it felt like I was talking about someone else. She was in tears too and just kept saying, "It will be OK, it will be OK."

The next few hours went by in a blur, with intermittent phone calls from mum, both of us somehow keeping it together to talk about the practicalities; I had to go home - I wanted to drive that day but knew I couldn't. Pete asked what I wanted him to do and I asked him to stay, so he did, and we went with Elle to the Chy bar where we sat drinking hot chocolate and watching the world go by. No-one else seemed to have a care in the world and it dawned on me that I didn't wear a virtual label to say that I was bereaved; no-one else would know unless they were told. We went back to the house and gradually I saw housemates and friends whom I had to tell, each time becoming more surreal than the first; it felt like I was telling a horrible story of something that had happened on TV and that I would soon be able to stop telling it. This, obviously, would never happen.

I remember such weird thoughts going through my mind; "This can't have happened, I've already lost Dad." "Was he pushed?" "Did he commit suicide?" and, above all, "How are we going to cope?"

Later on that evening I spoke to my boss and told him in a matter-of-fact way what had happened and that I wasn't going to be in work the next day and he arranged for someone to pick up my work things the next morning.

Pete and I watched a film, I can't remember which one, I don't think I really watched it. Then he left to go home and I wondered if that would be the last I would see of him.

I drove home the next day and kept wondering if "my brother has just died" would be a good enough excuse for speeding if I was pulled over! Every so often I would burst into tears - I must have looked like a crazy woman to anyone driving past! Somehow I made it home and I dreaded walking though that front door, getting odd flashbacks of how it must have been the previous morning when the police turned up at the front door to do the worst job they are probably ever trained to do. Mum had been worried about the "poor young chap" who wasn't able to hide that it was his first time doing this kind of visit and had been visibly upset.

I don't really remember the days that followed, only fragments: our living room looking like a flower shop, tons of pastel-coloured, flowery cards with various levels of heart-wrenching messages from friends and family, endless phone calls and hearing mum explain what had happened again and again, constant text messages as my social grapevine did its work. I recall our sombre visit to the funeral director where we had to choose a coffin from a catalogue - our black sense of humour feigning a chuckle at the 'picnic hamper' and selecting the first one that half stood out - it wasn't a decision to deliberate over after all. I remember horrible images in my mind when the man said that the coroner had advised that "the body wouldn't be suitable for viewing." Even now I catch myself sometimes wondering how he might have looked and I like to think he just looked a bit chilly.

I went back to Newquay for the weekend on the train (the longest journey of my life) and tried to be 'normal', going to a James Blunt concert (not a good gig when you're not feeling your happiest!), walking lots and trying to organise my thoughts and come to terms with what had happened.

114

Days just merged into one as arrangements were finalised and visitors came and went. The dreaded funeral was hideous but somehow I managed to do a reading between hyperventilating and feeling faint! So many people were there but I don't remember faces. David Hampshire was a diamond, conducting a dignified and positive service. The gathering at our house afterwards was quite pleasant and it was such a sunny day that it made people smile and be happy in the face of such adversity.

The anti-climax after the funeral meant that suddenly we were all alone; mum, Shaun and myself. I felt the gross unfairness of it all, how everyone would grieve for that week and then would be able to get on with their lives and forget about James. I felt bitter and angry with James that, having only just come to terms with Dad's death, here I was again with another uphill struggle. I knew it would get worse before it got better and I was right. I closed up completely, barely able to talk about it without anger and bitterness coming out, feeling terrified that it would happen to someone else I loved and that someone had it in for our family.

I found it hard to be around 'ignorant' people, especially in my job working with incapacity benefit claimants who often had nothing wrong with them more than a severe lack of motivation to do anything with their lives. What a waste, I thought, when James hadn't been able to live a long life. He hadn't been able to learn to drive, finish his degree, have a serious long-term relationship, children, a full-time job…but I also realised that fate plays a strange part in our lives; Mum confessed that she had never been able to imagine him making 'old bones', had never imagined him settling down and getting married as she could envisage for me.

115

Regarding the support I received, mum was and remains always there. I worry that I don't support her enough as I find it so hard to talk about when I know that sometimes she really wants to. I went to a counsellor about a month after James died, but she was useless and then I went again to face my anxieties and was given six sessions before the counsellor decided I was 'better' and signed me off. As a sibling, I feel forgotten sometimes (in a totally selfish way!) I think that there is a lot of support and help for parents but I have noticed that the natural response from most people when I tell them about what happened is "and how is your mum?" rather than asking me how I am. This is just an automatic response but does prove that it is not considered as 'bad' to lose a sibling as it is to lose a child, which I agree with to a point.

There is a line in 'Everybody's free to Wear Sunscreen' by Baz Luhrmann that goes 'Be nice to your siblings; they are the best link to your past and the people most likely to stick with you in the future. ' I feel very sad when I hear this as I know that my link has gone and that all my future memories will be built without James in them.

James and I didn't always see eye-to-eye, in a perfectly normal sibling animosity kind of way, but we did love each other dearly and had just started to have a grown-up understanding of each other, with the odd text being exchanged and having hugs when we saw each other. My only regret is that we didn't spend more time together and that I didn't get to know him more, but that was the way we were.

I view my future as a happy one, but with poignant moments where I know I will miss James' presence even more; my wedding day (I always hoped he would give me away after dad died), when my children are born (he would have been an amazing uncle - and babysitter!!!) and moments in my life in years to come when we would have been able to reminisce together, which will now not happen.

Today I can say that I feel happy with my life, and no longer bitter and twisted. I still struggle with the inevitable questions in new social situations, when siblings are mentioned. This seems to happen a lot because I don't live near my family. How I answer depends on my mood. I decided a while ago not to worry about causing embarrassment to people and I always answer directly now, explaining that my brother died and that I also have a stepbrother and a stepsister (always shuts them up!) I have learned that people are often just insensitive by nature and not to let it bother me.

My spiritual beliefs have strengthened and I have trained as a Reiki master since James died. I believe in an afterlife and that James and other family members watch over me, helping to guide me in life's choices. This gives me hope and comfort and I know that this will always be with me.

I like to think of myself as a positive person, who brings happiness to people, and I think, two years on, I am almost back there, but for a while I lost my personality and it was replaced by a horrible, bitter, negative and wounded soul who didn't see that bad things aren't planned for her and assumed that everything she touched would leave her. I am now 'me' again, with the extra experience of how to live with grief (great - something to put on my CV!) and the belief that we should live our lives as best we can, sometimes impulsively, sometimes in a planned fashion, but always with love and thought for those closest to us.

My relationship with mum has gone from strength to strength; we were always close but events over recent years have bonded us in a way that I would never have imagined possible. We have a dark and sometimes terrible sense of humour and I love the fact that we allow ourselves to live and laugh again. Mum is an absolute rock; she is incredibly strong and is a real role model for me. She has a way of being able to cheer me up and humble me if I am feeling sorry for myself. So if anything good can come from losing James in such a way, then this is it. I wouldn't ever dream of taking advantage of my lovely family and friends, as (using a phrase that comes up again and again) life is too short and I want to make the most of all the wonderful people in my life."

James' good friend Angela agreed to share with me her thoughts on how she was affected by the loss of James. She and James met when they both started a primary teaching degree at Brighton University. Ange has gone on to become a fully qualified teacher and has spent some considerable time on teaching assignments in Africa. She is currently teaching in Australia.

Ange came up with the novel idea of recording a conversation with her mother about her feelings regarding the loss; she then transcribed it and sent it to me. The following extracts give a good sense of the depth of her feelings and how she deals with them.

Maureen: How did you learn of his accident and how did you pass on the news to others?

Ange: I had a call from the police. James was due to come here at some point that summer and the police were asking me loads of questions about James because he was missing but at that time I didn't think anything of it.

118

I thought he might have stayed round someone else's and then after about three days I realised it was a bit strange. I remember calling him and thinking it's weird his phone's not even registering and that's when I got a bit suspicious.

I remember it was an evening and Andrea called and told me.

I didn't really understand – it was just something so far beyond what I ever thought would ever happen that at that point I couldn't even register in my mind that he was actually gone. That evening I slept in your bed – me, Gill (Ange's twin sister) and you; we made a big bed out on the side. I didn't sleep at all. I cried a lot. We were just hugging and crying.

Maureen: How has the loss affected you?

Ange: My initial reaction in terms of how it affected me was that I never thought I'd ever get over it and then I just thought, "That's my best friend that I've made, and I don't think I've ever had a better friend than him." For a little while I thought I didn't want to go back (to university) but I always knew I would go back because I think I believed James would want me to and that he wouldn't want me to stop doing my teaching course because he hadn't got the chance to finish it in a way, so I remember thinking I am definitely going to stay and everyone was offering me beds and things and I thought I'm always going to be OK. The first couple of times when I went back to Brighton I remember crying the first time I drove back – I couldn't go past Varley Halls [the Halls of residence where James and Ange lived]. Any time I went up there it made me feel really weird.

Maureen: How has your loss affected the way you feel about your own family?

Ange: At the time I remember thinking I don't want to let anyone go anywhere on their own. I remember specifically Gill going somewhere on a long drive; it might have been going up to Leeds or somewhere a couple of weeks later and me thinking "That could be the last time I see her" whereas beforehand it would never cross my mind to think that could be the last time I'd see someone. It just made me realise that life is very precious. It made me realise who was important to me like the people who were around, obviously the family, friends and the people who are going to be there for you for a long time, the people who can support you in something like that.

Maureen: Describe your own grief path and the way you were supported.

Ange: I couldn't put a point – I don't think there was ever a point where I started thinking "Oh you know it will be OK." Now, any time I think of James, I feel happy. I bought a ring – shortly before he died we went out and bought a ring for him together and I helped him choose it and I remember thinking when he died I really wanted something to remember him by as all his stuff had been taken from uni, and I remember thinking "Oh I haven't got anything" and I couldn't exactly ask for anything from Andrea or Shaun. I remember thinking that if I bought another ring the same as the one James bought I would have a little bit of James with me all the time. And every time I use the George Foreman grill or any of his mugs I think "Oh that's James."

I'd say now that my memory of him has got a lot weaker in that when it first happened I remember thinking, "but James is still so alive" and you know it's been two years and I can't really remember everything as clearly. It used to be like "we did this the other day and about a month ago we did that and we made up this dance" and now I can't remember so much about him so vividly, so I really like it when I see places...when I see that church in Brighton – always when I see that church in Brighton that we both lit candles – he lit one for his Dad and I lit one for his Dad and one for other people, Grandma and Grandad, I always think about James and I like it because it makes me take time out and actually think about him. It's so important to have that special place – definitely.

Maureen: Would any support have helped?

Ange: I think about that and I think it would be brilliant for certain people. I remember feeling at the time "just get over this - people have had a lot worse things happen and it was just my best friend and I should just get over it and I don't really deserve people talking to me about it." A book specifically addressing teenagers/young people and loss of friends would have been a help.

Maureen: How do you feel today as opposed to when the loss was new?

Ange: Just completely different – it's hard to think back to how I felt at that time. I still feel loss – I still feel upset sometimes when I think about what he may have gone on to achieve in life, particularly teaching; someone will say something and spark it off and I think "Oh James would have loved that." I only ever think about James in a happy way now. I think it's great that I still know his family – when I hear from Andrea...I think that's helped as well.

121

I guess the turning point in a way was when I started thinking "be positive about it rather than regretting" – yeah, I guess it's that initial grief, I guess everyone has to go through that – I don't think you can help it whether you try to feel in a positive way or not I think you'll always feel that massive pain. I literally just felt hollow. I remember always feeling sick; I just remember feeling hollow – I remember my head just not being able to think about anything else.

As for my spiritual beliefs, I remember thinking "I hope he's all right in heaven" because I believe in all the heaven and hell stuff and I assumed he'd be going there. And I remember at one point being like, "Oh it's so annoying that God can do nothing about good people that die", but not ever really blaming him or changing my faith at all.

Jenna Bailey is a writer who lost her sister in a motorway crash in 2007. In 2009, she wrote of her passage through grief and what it has taught her. She says, ⁴"Prior to losing Emma, I too was completely ignorant about the process and had no idea of the extent of the pain. I recall occasions when I must have been insensitive and I feel a sense of guilt about my lack of empathy." It is interesting that even in the depth of grief some people have the facility to think so much of the effect of their own grief on others.

Jenna says that one of the most valuable pieces of advice she was given was never to stop talking about her sister. Many people are afraid to mention the person who has died but this is a misplaced fear. Jenna's insight in this is remarkably sanguine.

⁵"I understood that people were simply afraid of upsetting me. In the past, when approaching a bereaved person, I too had thought it might be better not to bring the subject up, so

that I would not upset them. When Emma died, I quickly realised how misguided that fear was, at least in the way it related to me. Emma is in my mind all the time and there are no days when I do not think about her. For me it is impossible for someone to catch me off guard by mentioning her. You cannot remind me – I never forget."

Jenna also found herself longing for some sort of publicly recognised symbol that would demonstrate that she was bereaved. She says that she wanted something that would denote her sister's absence but that would also indicate to the people in her life that she was incapacitated by her grief and that she could barely perform even the most basic daily tasks.

Like Ange, Jenna found that the people who were helpful to her were the friends and family who were in pain themselves but generously acknowledged that she and Emma had been particularly close and who came to prop her up until she was able to support herself again.

Jenna shares a seminal message about loss of a sibling. She says, "I have discovered that grief is not something I had to go through, but rather something that I have to learn to live with. Grief seeps into every part of me and I will own it for the rest of my life. The pain, the longing, the sadness – they are all elements of the new me, a person dramatically altered by my experience. Although Emma is dead, she is far from gone. I will continue to find new ways to incorporate her into my life. It is a redefinition of our relationship, not an end to it."

[4, 5, 6] Copyright Jenna Bailey, 2009. First published in *You, The Mail on Sunday* 25 January 2009, used by permission of the Wylie Agency (UK) Limited

I admire the capacity that Jenna has to view her loss as a new relationship. This is an approach that I had not considered before. I am not sure I can apply it to a mother/child relationship in quite the same way, as a sibling loss is by its nature different from a parental loss. Having said that, however, I think that it is another example of how we come to absorb grief in myriad different ways and choose whichever work best for us as individuals. Stella, Ange and Jenna all express their loss and their grief paths in different ways. What they all have in common though, is an acknowledgment that time heals the worst of the wounds and that the precious nature of the support of family and friends cannot be overstated. Indeed the precious nature of life itself becomes heightened by the experience of traumatic grief.

If you are a step parent, how do you deal with grief for a child who was not your blood relative? It is hard enough to blend as a family after divorce or death of a spouse, let alone cope with experiencing the loss of one of the children.

In some respects, stepfamilies are 'born of loss'. Whether formed by separation and divorce, as most are today, or the death of a parent, it is clear that loss of some type is the precursor to stepfamily life.

The complex feelings emanating from both divorce and death have their source in loss; they both give rise to a grief process, which has many levels for various members of the family.

Fortunately, the gradual blending together of our families after Shaun and I met in 2000 did not, as I recall, cause any specific problems. Shaun and I were very careful to take our relationship slowly so as to consider the feelings of all our offspring; my children Stella and James and his son and daughter, Janine and Mark. They were all in their teens when Shaun and I met. At the time of James' passing, none of the children were living with us. Stella moved to Cornwall in 2004 and Mark was staying with his grandparents locally. Janine lived with her mother at that time. James had been at university for a year and we were used to living on our own, most of the time.

What is particularly notable is that since James' passing, I have not discussed his death or our subsequent grieving with either Janine or Mark. We have touched on the subject around the anniversary and during the time we were campaigning for safety improvements at Kingston riverside, but we have not had specific conversations in the same way that Stella and I have talked through our emotions from time to time. The children had not spent much time together at all, so James must have seemed relatively remote to both Janine and Mark – there was no animosity between any of them, but they simply did not know each other very well.

We all share good and harmonious relationships now, but there is a blank space in communication which, after all this time, feels too difficult to raise. I do not think I have ever discouraged discussion about James and what happened to him, it is simply the case that there was not sufficient closeness in our relationships at the time for either Mark or Janine to approach me. I have never intentionally discouraged conversation about James; it simply hasn't happened. Perhaps it does not need to. Perhaps it is just too painful a topic for them to visit, but equally I think they are sensitive to my feelings surrounding James and do not wish to upset me, or their father, by bringing up the subject. It is a tricky area in which to find the right path to follow.

Stella and I are very open with each other about our feelings and I think that has helped us both over the most terrible times of our grieving. Equally, Shaun and I communicate well about our feelings too.

James was 15 when Shaun and I met and at that time he was a typically uncommunicative teenager. He was very protective of the household and of me; I was relatively newly divorced. Unfortunately my ex husband died in 2002 which necessarily added another dimension to all our relationships. Shaun was placed in a difficult position at that time when my children were grieving the loss of their father at the same time as assimilating the fact that I had a new relationship. I think it is a credit to Stella, James, Janine and Mark that individually they coped so well with the profound changes that went on during this period.

I believe all the children had accepted our relationship by the time Shaun and I married, and thus it was even more devastating that we lost James so soon after our wedding. It was dreadful for us all to be toppled from the elation of the wedding day to the depths of despair within such a short time, and it was quite shattering to our new stepfamily set up. One of the worst aspects was having many of the same people attending our wedding and James' funeral just six weeks later.

The assumption seems to be that the stepfamily, unlike the biological family, cannot possibly understand or feel the depth of the loss. I would challenge that because it is impossible to measure feelings of loss and there should never be a sense of competition in grief. Janine and Mark lost a stepbrother whom they had hardly begun to know. We should be aware of the emotions of surviving siblings who are not blood relations of the child who has died, but it is so hard in the early days to reach out to anyone outside the immediate family and I think there is a tendency for them to be neglected. Certainly I feel that because Shaun and I had a new marriage, some people struggled to know whether they should acknowledge the loss of James directly with Shaun and they had a tendency to ask how I was doing all the time, rather than remembering than he was grieving too. This commonly happens to siblings as well.

For step parents the grief experience is a precarious journey as they try to balance the needs of their spouses, their own feelings, and the feelings of their children, biological and non-biological. It is a time when communication is of the utmost importance. In hindsight, I wish we had all been able to sit down together and talk about James in the early stages of loss.

During a stepfamily's formation both adults and children are dealing with the major grief tasks of preserving the past and establishing a new future. When this balancing act is skewed, for example in our case where a child has been lost and the family dynamic altered, it is difficult to see how the fragments can be brought together again. I am sure it helped Shaun and me immeasurably to have time and space in our grieving because we did not have children still living at home, but it was unhelpful to the children themselves who were unable to express their grief with us on a day to day basis.

In the early weeks and months after losing James, our house was very quiet. Once the initial flurry of visitors in the immediate aftermath of the event had passed, we spent a lot of time on our own. This was both a good and a bad thing. For me, it was good to be able to have time to devote to working out how to grieve. For Shaun, it must have been very hard for him to see me day after day struggling to maintain some semblance of normality.

It was a long time before people felt they could socialise and visit us again with any degree of spontaneity. We discovered that we always had to take the lead in contacting other people and sometimes the effort of doing so was simply too much. But at least we had the choice.

Shaun once said to me, "Your grief is harder than mine because James was your child."

To an extent this is true because James was a product of my body, I helped create him and I carried him, so of course we had the maternal/filial bond of mother and son. But I believe that Shaun carries not only his own grief, but that of his children who have not expressed it. I think he has learned about grief the hard way through living with a grieving wife.

As Stella's stepfather, he carries another separate grief in being unable to comfort her in the way that her biological father could.

Knowing Shaun as I do, I can understand how deeply the loss affects him. Shaun lost a stepson with whom he had a good relationship that was in its formative stages, and he has been denied the opportunity to develop that relationship. This is another facet of grief that I think is not necessarily acknowledged by people who do not appreciate or understand the depth of loss that is felt by a stepparent.

Being newly married when James died, we had a great sense of trying to sustain our good relationship even in the face of this dreadful, unexpected adversity, and whichever spouse was feeling stronger at any given moment wanted to make everything better for the other.

Shaun did a good job of learning that a song, a date or some other stimulus could trigger my grief and my mood could change quickly. He learned that sometimes I need to experience my grief with the minimum of distraction and he has always been brilliant at giving me the space I need.

I think it is fair to say that searching for the reasons I may be low is his task, and honest answers are my best response. It is easy to say you feel OK to please the other person but it is more truthful to be open with them with an explanation why you may be feeling particularly fragile at a given time.

There is a sense of isolation for the stepfamily if, as in our case, the children have not known each other for long or been raised together. We expect a lot of our children when blending a family. Just because we, the adults, have formed a loving relationship does not mean that our children will like each other on sight. It would be naive to assume that the children will all get on and make friends. But the signs were that all four of our children would share amicable, if not close, relationships and it is very sad that the relationships cannot continue with the same dynamic because we have lost James.

My relationship with my stepchildren is probably a less involved one that it would have been if I had been part of their lives in their formative years. They have a good rapport with their mother and grandparents. I have never been made anything other than welcome within the family but I do not feel it appropriate to quiz them about their feelings about James; it feels as though it would be too intrusive.

Stella had been living in Cornwall for a year when James died; she had a full time job and was sharing a house with some friends, and thoroughly enjoying the lifestyle in the West Country. She had also just met Pete - who is now her husband - and although I know she would have come home to stay and support me if I had asked her, we discussed it and agreed it really was not an option. In fact, I think I would have found it harder to have her at home and cope with her grief as well as my own.

Poor Stella, each time she came up from Cornwall to visit she was hit anew by the raft of memories associated with her home town, and I am sure it was very difficult for her to contend with worrying about me and how I was doing as well.

But Stella says that for her, it was easier to disassociate herself from what had happened because of the distance and the fact that none of her friends had met James; indeed, most of her colleagues did not even know she had a brother. She will acknowledge now that she side-lined her grief because it was easier at the time, and over the years she has gradually been able to process it in her own way, but it has been very much a case of one step forward and two steps back for her. She recently told me, "You know mum, I don't remember 2006 at all, yet I was working and functioning, but there is a great gap in my memory banks." I know how she feels.

He is Gone

You can shed tears that he is gone
or you can smile because he has lived.
You can close your eyes and pray that he will come back
or you can open your eyes and see all he has left.
Your heart can be empty because you can't see him
or you can be full of the love you shared.
You can turn your back on tomorrow and live yesterday
or you can be happy for tomorrow because of yesterday.
You can remember him and only that he's gone
or you can cherish his memory and let it live on.
You can cry and close your mind,
be empty and turn your back
or you can do what he would want:
smile, open your eyes, love and go on.

Adapted from original by David Harkins 'She is Gone'

Chapter 7

How is Your Grief? The First Five Years

The grief path, road, route, journey - call it what you will -
has many descriptions and analogies that all have merit for
individuals seeking to find an approximately timetabled
layout for the working through of grief. The immensity of
the initial shock and trauma is impossible even to begin to
assimilate; it is just too vast.

When James first died, I can remember asking out loud
where on earth I could put my grief. It was massive, all
encompassing and dreadful in its intensity.
I couldn't see how I could possibly take something so
enormous, so utterly life-changing, into my everyday
existence. The greatest components of my grief were shock
and bewilderment that such a thing could have happened.
The oft repeated question 'Why?' as for all of us, remains
unanswered.

A Swiss friend of mine uses an expression for extreme
sadness that translates literally as 'carrying a stone on your
heart'. Initially, that stone replaced my heart, and each beat
and every breath felt as heavy as lead.

As the days passed, I began to visualise my grief as a huge
rock, and my desire was for time to accelerate, to chip away
at that rock, until it became a stone, and ultimately, I hoped,
a pebble. But I have learned that this process cannot be
rushed; it will take as long as it takes, there are no short
cuts, there is no magic chisel to whittle away the layers.

After the first year or so of loss, I recorded in my journal
that the rock was on its way to being a stone, still heavy on
my heart but more manageable day by day.

Of course, there are many obstacles that cause the rock to assume greater proportions again – birthdays, anniversaries, holidays – but each time one of these is faced, it is placed in 'yesterday' rather than 'tomorrow 'and I like to imagine that this causes another little shower of stone chips to fall. The presence of the rock has given me the capacity to feel greater compassion for others. I believe that the mutual exchange of empathy and support via the other bereaved parents I have met increases my own ability to deal with my personal grief. As parents, we reach out and are reached out to in return.

Collectively, we have strengths that the non-bereaved parent cannot begin to understand.

The future begins to look a little more attainable, more bearable. Ideally, it is a future where our children live on in our minds, ever present but not subsuming us to the extent that we cannot function. Resilience, strength from our memories, human nature itself, and the desire to behave in the way our children would want us to, all push us forward, however reluctantly, step by step. We slowly emerge from the black heart of despair, blinking at the chinks of light that warm our rocks of grief.

I currently view my own rock as having changed its character, from being a flat, grey, heavy chunk of matter to a lighter, more porous and colourful piece of stone.

Years ago, whenever we visited the coast, here or abroad, my children and I would pick up a few stones that had been smoothed by the sea. These had to fulfil certain criteria; they had to be tactile, preferably sun warmed, and of a size that would fit comfortably in the palm. We called them our 'thinking stones', and we all took to using them the way some cultures use worry beads.

I habitually carry one of these 'thinking stones' in my pocket. Every so often I clasp it in my hand, roll it around and warm it, and it has gradually acquired the identity of my grief. I know that one day, in the future, however long it takes, this will represent the size of my grief. It will fit into the palm of my hand and no longer be an insurmountable challenge. It will be smooth and curved without the jagged edges of early mourning.

It will represent the softening of the harsh reality of what has to be faced on a daily basis. Its tiny mineral chips will reflect light instead of absorbing darkness. The stone or pebble will, in time, be replaced by a smooth tumble stone.

At the end of the first year I noted that it remains my daily quest to work as positively as I can through my loss and to come out the other side with something approaching calm acceptance of that which cannot be changed. My path was set in positivity at an early stage.

From the start, I read avidly and sought examples of evidence that the terrible gut wrenching, searing pain of early bereavement would subside.

I found it cathartic to write and by expressing my emotions in the written word, my emotions became more level and less of a rollercoaster. Looking back at my journal is helpful to measure progress and in 2007 I wrote:

"The other day, my TCF contact asked me in an email: 'How is your grief journey?'

His question set me thinking and I realised that in recent months, I have not devoted much time to assessing how I am doing. The time has gone by both in an instant and an age.

The tearing agony of early grief has gradually given way to an ever present, dull, background ache that sits somewhere alongside my heartbeat.

We have managed to get through birthdays, Christmas, holidays and our own noteworthy personal dates, and in each case the second round has been easier than the first. As we approach the anniversary date again, it looms on the calendar like a massive obstacle to be surmounted, but with the experience of last year, I know that we will cross that particular Rubicon when it comes.

Initially, I remember giving much thought to the archetypal 'stages of grief' that I read about, but as time goes by I begin to understand that these are totally individual and that for each of us, it takes as long as it takes.

As for acceptance, it is imperceptibly beginning to find its place in my psyche. On an everyday level, I can and do accept that my son is no longer alive, but he lives on in my mind, still 19, still smiling and still living a full life somewhere in a parallel universe. If that represents acceptance, then I can live with it."

(Looking back, I am amazed that I could write this at such an early stage after we lost James. It seems incredible now that I could have had the arrogance to believe that I was accepting what had happened.

I think it is more likely that at this stage, I had begun to absorb the shock. These days, I view absorption as a better description than acceptance).

I went on to say: "Anticipation has gradually returned to my life. I can look forward to events and enjoy them when they arrive, something that seemed impossible at the outset.

I can feel sort of happy, although I accept that the happiness I feel now is not the same as that which I felt before and cannot be otherwise.

Time has settled into 'before' and 'after' and I often have difficulty remembering in which period certain events happened. My perception of time seems permanently altered.

My concentration has improved. In recent months I have had little choice but to concentrate on my work because of changes in the workplace, and this has definitely shifted my emphasis away from grieving, which is perhaps not a bad thing.

Nearly two years down the line, I can feel lucky; lucky that I had my son for 19 years, lucky that his death was an accident and lucky that I do not have anyone to blame. I am fortunate too in being able to focus on effecting changes at the riverside where he died, so I know that in future, such accidents will be prevented.

My sorrow remains unaltered, particularly when I think of all he will be missing from his own, would-have-been, future. But perhaps his eternal life, wherever it is, will far surpass the life he would have led had he not died when he did. There must be some consolation there.

If I examine my grief now, I see something that has become manageable rather than all consuming. I live with it, because I have no other choice and it is a permanent attachment to my life.

I am not particularly brave or courageous, but I believe that I have been given the strength to do this – to live through this most appalling event and come through the other side.

There is no choice but to continue life after loss, however hard that is.

Throughout my journey so far, I have gathered as many tools as possible to aid me in my progression and to be able to work through my grief in as positive a way as I can manage.

I have read and written a great deal, I have talked, I have listened, I have wept and I have at times eaten, drunk and smoked too much and tasted the bitter gall of despair in the dead of night. I have benefited in some indefinable way from counselling.

I sought a spiritual path, exploring the concept of 'life after life' and this gives me a great deal of comfort and the strong conviction that I will be reunited, not just with James, but with my other lost loved ones at the time of my own passing.

I have been supported by and given support to my dear daughter and my lovely husband. Yes, I feel lucky.

My 'after' friendships with other bereaved parents perhaps provide the best mutual support and certainly the greatest understanding of what it is really like to live with loss on an everyday level. I hope that I too am a compassionate friend; certainly I feel that tragedy leads one to be generally more compassionate.

My loss has caused me to re-evaluate my priorities in life and trivial upsets have ceased to worry me. The enormity and untimely loss of one's child is immeasurable. What else can really matter after such a loss?

A flat tyre on the car, queues in the supermarket; such things are irrelevant now and can be easily managed. This attitude is echoed by Mary Berry, who lost her son Will in a vehicle accident many years ago. She said, "You learn to live with it and say 'Thank you' for having him. After Will I can drop a cut-glass bowl and just turn away and sweep it up and put it in the bin. Once you hit big things you realise your family is the most important thing you've got."

I look to the future now in a completely different way. I am definitely more fearful for those close to me – after all who better than I to know that life can be turned upside down in an instant – but I try not to dwell on this and remain positive about others' longevity.

In the early days of grief it is impossible to look beyond the next day, sometimes the next hour or even one's own next breath. But as time passes it is possible to look forward again and embrace your life as a participant rather than an onlooker.

Two years after James' death, I wrote, "Here I am, two-years- old in 'new normality' – how does it feel? I am walking, talking, loving, thinking, feeling, functioning and living this new life to the best of my ability.

At first, I felt small and insignificant, as though the event had somehow compacted the self I knew, with the weight of grief pushing its way down through me so that I struggled to breathe and to have the strength and confidence to rise above it.

But, with determination, I have surmounted many of the obstacles of early grieving to restore myself to a reasonable facsimile of who I was before.

Of course, I can never be that 'before' woman again. I, as the mother of two living children, am a person of the past, but the new version of that woman is becoming more familiar and actually, I quite like her! She is more compassionate, more positive and more driven to get as much as possible out of her life. She is learning to make the most of any opportunities and seek out ways to grow, both emotionally and spiritually. She is prepared to acknowledge when she needs help and to accept support willingly.

One of the most positive results to come from the devastation of a life taken too soon is a greater appreciation of life itself and an increased awareness of how precious and fleeting it is in reality. This leads to a shift in perspective and the realisation of what is truly important in the grand scheme of things.

I try not to spend time thinking 'What if ..?' or 'What would he look like/be doing now?' I prefer to concentrate on everything that James achieved in his 19 years, both practically and emotionally. The legacy of his life is made up of all the memories of him shared by everyone who knew and loved him."

My observations on how to cope with being bereaved and how to present an acceptable face to the world on a day to day basis are useful tools in a griever's armoury. I observed the following:

"You learn to put on a daily mask that allows you to function in a near normal state around other people. You develop a shell to allow comments made by unthinking people such as: 'He/she is in a better place'; 'You will get over it'; 'It's time to move on', to simply wash over you.

140

You quickly realise that the people who truly appreciate what you are going through are those who are experiencing it themselves. This is well illustrated by a friend who said to me, 'The only way I could understand what you are going through would be by walking five miles in your shoes.' How true. The loss of a child is different from other bereavement that we may experience, such as the loss of a parent, because it is untimely.

You are drawn to other bereaved parents for support, which somehow evolves into a mutual propping up that is incredibly helpful and leads to new and meaningful friendships. You may benefit from counselling, although I believe that this should not begin too soon. I found Cruse Bereavement Care counselling very helpful. I started around nine months after James died and was lucky to bond with my counsellor. Initially I resisted the idea of counselling as I as defensive about my own need for it, but it turned out to be of inestimable value.

There is a raft of bereavement literature on the Internet and in books and it is incredibly useful to draw on what you need for your particular circumstances.

You may find that you use your own tools – writing is cathartic and it can be very beneficial to keep a journal, particularly in the first year. Otherwise, using creative expression in art, crafts, or perhaps exercise, can help to express grief in safe and beneficial ways.

You also learn a kind of fatigue compassion, as you realise that others, be they family or friends, often simply do not know what to say to you – and you will become tired of making allowances for these people, even whilst you appreciate that you yourself would have been one of them before you lost your child.

I have come to loathe the words 'At least...', even though I use them myself. You may hear: 'At least he didn't suffer'; 'At least you had him for 19 years' and, perhaps worst of all, 'You are doing so well; I have no idea how I would cope.'

There is a temptation to respond, 'Actually, I have no idea how I cope either; I just don't have a choice!'

Unfortunately, some friendships will be irrevocably altered as people cannot cope with what you are going through. If I am being uncharitable, I wonder if they think bereavement might be contagious and see me as some kind of grim reaper.

On the other hand, you are likely to find support from people you least expected to be able to prop you up, which kind of balances it out. Extended family relationships, such as my tentative developing relationship with my stepchildren, could undoubtedly be set back by such an event, but this – at least in my experience further along the line – is not irrevocable.

You will be told how brave you are; little does everyone know that you are actually scared witless at the thought of living the rest of your life without your child and being unable to enjoy the events in their future that they have been denied. But you will find yourself projecting the image that is expected of you. Society dictates that you conform in grieving, as in other areas of life.

When you begin to read bereavement literature, it is comforting to know that however crazy you think you are being, especially in the first year, whatever you are doing will have been done by someone before you and can therefore be filed in the category 'normal behaviour by bereaved parent'. For example, ringing your child's mobile phone, sending him/her e-mails, seeing them in the street/supermarket/petrol station; all these are quite *normal*, as indeed is putting the iron in the fridge and the milk in the oven.

There are no rules and there is no textbook; it seems that anything that can help in whatever way is acceptable provided it does not get out of hand within your own personal bounds.

As the weeks and months slip slowly by, however, the crazy incidents gradually become fewer and are insidiously and reluctantly replaced by a growing absorption of the irrefutable fact of the loss."

The third year of loss saw quite a change in my attitude towards my grieving and a far greater insight into the process. I wrote:

"I have found this year to be markedly different from the first and second years.

I have approached the grieving process as a challenge to be met with as much positive input as possible, whilst trying to continue living in a purposeful way despite the shattering sudden loss of my son.

One of the best things to come out of year three is an awareness of the return of my self belief and confidence. In the early days of grief, our personalities are totally poleaxed by what has happened and this manifests itself in a lack of confidence that renders us incapable of performing as we had before our loss. One way I have tackled this has been to try new projects. Last year I learned how to practise Reiki.

This year, I took a college course in the jointly taught subjects of anatomy/physiology and holistic massage, leading to the appropriate qualifications.

I took the course with a work colleague who became a firm friend – incidentally, the first new friend I made post bereavement. I found a sense of enlivening freedom in the class of not being perceived as a bereaved parent. During the course, there were a couple of occasions where I could have mentioned or discussed my loss. I chose not to and I did not feel guilty of a sin of omission. It was surprisingly liberating to make that choice.

The tutors, however, knew of my loss and were extremely empathetic. They were very supportive and encouraged my determination to qualify. In particular, I found one tutor to be a remarkably sensitive and caring man. He wrote some wonderful words to me after we had spoken of James:

"When I was a little boy I remember saying to my Grandpa whom I loved very much, that I wanted him never to die. He said to me then, and at his bedside when he did finally pass away, that *children are the messages parents and grandparents send to a time that they themselves will not see.* When one survives one's children one might imagine being left to carry that message oneself."

These words set me thinking. Perhaps the fact that James' life was cut short at the age of 19 means that I have to pick up the baton that was set as a pattern for *his* life, and continue to live my own life to compensate and to fill the gap left by what he would have achieved.

Given that in a normal lifespan he should have lived many more years, the onus is now on me to pack into living as much as I possibly can, so as not to waste the life he cannot now live. I believe I owe it to James not to live my life in grief, misery and despair, but to utilise whatever means are at my disposal to live as full and as content a life as possible.

The third year has made the concept of happiness a reality again. The grey mantle of early grief has dissipated and settled into an enduring feeling of sadness, which occupies a place further towards the background of my mind. The downside of this, though, is that there are times when I feel that the presence that was James is becoming too remote. It is like looking at a slightly out of focus photograph, where the edges are indistinct.

I suddenly realised this year that I have regained my former liking for bright colours in my wardrobe. New grief clothes itself in insignificance, but I feel able to put aside the dull browns and muted greys that I initially presented to the world.

I believe that looking forward instead of backwards is a preferable route to take in dealing with loss; sidelining negative emotions in favour of a renewed sense of trust in the Fates and a belief that what happened to us was not the forerunner of a preordained run of bad events."

By the fourth year of loss, I found I could articulate my feelings more broadly, focusing less on being a bereaved parent and more on how life is affected by general grieving.

I used a quote by deaf-blind Helen Keller to introduce my thoughts at the fourth anniversary: "The hands of those I meet are dumbly eloquent to me. The touch of some hands is an impertinence. I have met people so empty of joy that when I clasped their frosty fingertips it seemed as if I were shaking hands with a north-east storm.

Others there are whose hands have sunbeams in them, so that their grasp warms my heart."

The words suggest that Helen Keller was ultra sensitive to the nuances of expression she encountered through touch. To me, this echoes the extra emotional and physical sensitivity and awareness that gradually develops through living with loss.

Like many others who have lost a loved one, I initially felt the bleak despair of an apparently insurmountable challenge – the will to live a meaningful existence in the wake of loss.

I believe that the trauma of loss causes a major re-evaluation of precisely what life means to all of us as individuals. An accident that means that your loved one is here one second and gone the next is the most dreadful shock to the system, and it remains impossible to find the words to describe the devastating, gut-wrenching horror that accompanies such an event. Indeed, our own loss led to my being utterly 'empty of joy' and 'having frosty finger tips.' However, I will not dwell on the horrendous early days of grieving, as they are thankfully behind me and I feel almost sane again.

From the perspective of four years into the journey, the view is very different as I look along the road of what remains of my life – hopefully a good, long road! It is possible to emerge from the deaf-blind darkness of raw grief back into the arena of daylight.

Since the outset I have held a dread of reaching the Pearly Gates myself and having nothing new to tell James about my life after he left us. This is where Helen Keller's quotation begins to make more sense.

These days, I am much more aware of the importance and impact of hands and touch than I was prior to James' death. Our hands are vital to us and yet we take the many ways we use them for granted – for practical tasks, for expressing emotion, for clasping, for a reassuring pat on the shoulder, for shielding our eyes from sights we would prefer not to see, for prayer, in praise through applause and for reaching out to each other with compassion and comfort.

"The touch of some hands is an impertinence" is a good analogy for the way in which others can ride roughshod over grief, particularly early on, when they can thoughtlessly say things that intimate that you should be 'over it' and 'back to your old self' with apparently hardly a thought for what you must be going through. It takes time to build a mental armoury against such occurrences.

James was undoubtedly one of Helen Keller's quoted others "whose hands have sunbeams in them, so that their grasp warms my heart." His infectious smile went with the affectionate warmth of his 'special hugs' and I believe he himself had healing hands. It is not too fanciful to say that I often feel his presence working through my own hands when I am carrying out therapies and I believe his energy fuels my own to keep me positive and strong. It is impossible to accept that such a vivacious life force as he possessed does not still find ways to express itself and I find this very comforting.

There is much written in bereavement literature about finding the gift in loss. At first, this seems the most preposterous and unachievable idea, because all that can be felt is the searing pain of grief and its agonies must be both confronted and worked through before one can hope to reach a measure of peace and acceptance. The timescale for this is impossible to specify, and perhaps some people will never reach a level of acceptance that sits comfortably with them. However, I have never wanted to remain "empty of joy" and have constantly and mindfully sought out the most positive aspects that I can find from my loss. I focus on the fact that at the time he died, James was a happy young man and our relationship was good.

James died in an accident that should have been eminently preventable and the focus of my attention in the early years of loss was to ensure that safety measures were instituted at the place where he lost his life. I do not underestimate the positive effect this project had on my grief path, for I felt by the end of it that I had achieved something tangible to represent James, and his legacy will prevent others going through the trauma that we have experienced.

After four years, I feel placed to express, through personal opinion developed through my own experience, some of the things that I view as helpful or unhelpful in approaching grief:

- Grief should be expressed in whatever form gives you release and comfort, be it reading, writing, talking, painting, seeking counselling, following your spiritual or religious belief system or giving vent to a primal scream on top of a mountain or in the middle of a field – take whichever route is helpful.

- Grief should not be repressed, regardless of your fear of embarrassing others. If you want to cry, go ahead and cry. Don't try to lock grief away, because it will find its way out somehow.

- There are times when grief renders you numb, switched off and silent; I view this as nature's way of providing a break from the sheer effort of getting through the process.

- Grief should not mean being afraid to talk about the person who has gone. Well-meaning others fear that they will upset you if they mention the person who has died. My response to this has always been, "How on earth do you think I could be any more upset?!" However, finding a tactful way to convey this can be rather difficult. Pointing out that it helps me to remember James is helpful.

- Grief should not be competitive. Is my grief any easier or harder to cope with than that of the parents who have tragically lost serving soldiers in Afghanistan?

- A parent's grief does not necessarily vary according to how their child died

- Grief should not and cannot be disowned. Denial of grieving is actually quite futile; if you do not give vent to your grief, it will eat away at you and fill you with bitterness and pain.

- A healer who knew nothing of my history told me that I was carrying a great deal of pain and sorrow. She went on to say that I should "let the pain go, but accept and live with the sorrow." Whilst I do not fully understand how that can be achieved, her words have stayed with me and in themselves they make sense. The pain of new loss is a searing entity.

The pain of older loss equates to a dull ache that ultimately becomes less noticeable – although it is ever present.

- Grief can increase your compassion and empathy. Early grieving is so introspective that there is little room for anyone or anything else. Gradually though, the tunnel vision recedes and you find you become far more aware of what is happening around you and you may find yourself able to support others as you slowly move towards the light.

- The introspection of grief can lead to your giving more thought to various complementary healing therapies and if you have the interest, you may find that you come to recognise and learn a wider spectrum of ways of dealing with negative emotion.

- There is comfort in knowing that the grief process consists of emotions that are 'normalised' by the frequency with which they are experienced by individuals; hence they are accepted and therefore become more acceptable and tolerable.

- Railing against the fates that have conspired to cause your loss is satisfying, but ultimately absorption of that which has happened needs to take place for your future peace of mind, and this is very difficult to take on board at the beginning of the process.

There is also solace in following what, as time passes, become the personally tailored rituals of grief, which develop into part of the observance of special dates.

It may be that in coming years the need will be less, or it may be that the need to repeat the same actions will always be there, but the point is that it doesn't matter; these observances are highly individual and personal to your own circumstances and that is all that counts. I believe that intuition shows you the most comfortable way to deal with such days and the innate wisdom that we all possess should be heeded to know how best to proceed. Experience has taught me that the lead up to and anticipation of the anniversary day is actually worse than the date itself. July is, for me, the longest month of the year.

The fourth year of loss surprised me with its intensity of feeling. There were times when I have suddenly been dropped back into the well of despair I recall from the beginning, but equally there were moments when I can honestly say I have experienced great joy. The return of optimism to my psyche and confidence to my personality are most welcome"

The fifth year saw a further shift in my grief path and the desire to assess and analyse the passage of five years. At this time, I wrote:

"As we approach the fifth anniversary of our loss, I have come to realise that this time holds a special significance. I have learned that we all grieve in different ways. It has taken me the past five years to fully absorb the premise of grief as an utterly individual process.

So – what is different about the five year anniversary?

For me, five years is time to step up to the mark and wholly confront the reality of the finality of the loss. This is a lonely way station on the grief route and the acceptance of arriving at such a place is hard won. Assimilating the fact that you will never again speak your child's name and get a direct response from him or her is one of the toughest boulders on the rocky road. As time passes, your child's name is mentioned less and less by others and that is also very hard to accept.

As others have before me, I draw parallels between the first five years of loss and the first five years in a child's life. The start is a blind, naive, fumbling, stumbling affair as one struggles to comprehend arriving into a jagged, noisy, discordant world.

But, somehow, survive we do. The first year passes, that crazy time of re-learning how to hold a cohesive thought, how to breathe and move and take baby steps to walk. At first, the bereaved parent fails to realise how widespread the ripple effect of their loss is. This is something that I felt more in the second year, as I was able to step back a little and review the way in which we were now relating to our family, extended family and friends. All our relationships have, to some degree, been irrevocably altered by our loss. There is a void that can never be filled, especially at significant times such as birthdays and Christmas.

Holidays and special occasions are particularly difficult without that special individual's input. It is very hard to feel celebratory without concomitant guilt at enjoying occasions in the absence of those who are missing. Over time, as I reviewed his 19 years and how fully he lived them, I began to be able to feel that it was better to have had James for that time and lost him, than never to have had him at all.

When I first began to read of grief and grieving as a bereaved parent, I shied away from anything that spoke of the 'gift' of loss, or 'choices to heal', for I felt too raw and hurt to consider that anything positive could come out of such a sudden and tragic loss. I will admit to feeling resentful that such a loss had happened to me until I read of others saying, 'Why not me?' instead of 'Why me?' and I began to believe that our paths are chosen for us at a level with which we can cope.

If I can find a gift in my loss, it is this: The love and joy of knowing James for nearly 20 years inspires me to continue to live my life to the full, not only for him, or indeed for myself, but for all those around me whose love and support I value and appreciate.I have learned to have insight into my grief and to try always to turn it to the positive rather than the negative. I have learned to accept that the experience of grief will stay with me until I, too, pass to the next plane, wherever and whenever that may be.

Perhaps one of the most important insights I have taken on board in the past five years is that healing and recovery from such a traumatic loss require a conscious decision by us to actually want to recover. There are times that grief cries out to be revisited and I liken this to taking it out of its box, examining it, wearing it, being with it in whatever way feels right, before putting it back again and moving forward. The box is constantly there, sitting peripherally and I accept that it will always be there.

With all the evidence that I have gathered through my own passage along the grief path, through reading and communicating with other bereaved parents, it is an obvious conclusion that five years is indeed a significant milestone. A five-year-old child stands, walks, talks and reasons. A five-year-old child is capable of deep emotion, be it happy or sad, and a 5-year-old child is learning about the passage of time and the anticipation of events. A five-year-old child possesses a degree of independence.

As a 5-year-old bereaved parent, I can relate to all the above and would add that I feel as though I am achieving a degree of independence from my grief that I could not have envisaged at the outset.

The weight of the pain of loss does not diminish, but it becomes an acceptably loaded burden to bear. The scale and enormity of loss does not change, but the way in which is can be absorbed into present and future life slowly and subtly alters with the passage of time."

Note to James:

Years ago, when you were just a little boy, maybe five or six, you saw an oily puddle on the tarmac in the park. I watched as you peered at the colours in it, prodded it with a stick, looked at it this way and that in puzzlement, before you turned to me and said, uncertainly, "Mummy, what's this? It looks like a rainbow, which fell out of the sky." And when I told you gently, "No sweetheart, it's not a rainbow; it is just reflections in the mix of oil and water, catching the sunlight," your bottom lip quivered, your eyes filled with tears, and you could only be consoled with a hug.

Your reaction seemed disproportionate to the event, but with the clearcut beliefs of the child you were, you were extremely upset.

The disappointment of that moment, set aside but never forgotten, is just a minuscule fraction of how missing you feels today, five years on.

For James - Past, Present, Future

We loved you, and
You loved us.
I wondered today
About your lifespan's 19 years,
How you grew from a vulnerable babe,
Totally dependent on those around you,
To become the unique person you were –
Independent, complex, strong,
Beautiful and amazing,
Balanced on the threshold of manhood.
Just another boy's life,
Filled with myriad experiences,
That make up our day to day existence,
And through it all you wove
A thread of unconditional love,
Amongst the laughter and the crises
That we shared,
There was never any doubt
How much you cared.
You gave us some hard times,
We gave you some hard times,
But always, your light shone through your smile.
How have we survived without you?
Somehow we have stumbled through the days,
Weaving our memories around us like a cloak,
To shield us from the pain of sudden loss.
Imperceptibly, the darkness has thinned
To the pearly greyness of an older grief,
With glimmers of light that inspire us
To move forward as and when we will,
Guided by your lively spirit.
This is your endless legacy.
We love you, and
You love us.

Andrea Corrie, 2005

155

Chapter 8

Are You Still Grieving? Beyond Five Years

My dear DSN friend Karen Ligtermoet asked, "I wonder what it is that enables some people to cope better than others. The love is no less and the loss no less significant and life changing but there seems to be such a difference in the way that people process their loss."

It is an interesting thought for there is no rulebook when it comes to grief and grieving. As parents, we are not given a rulebook in the delivery room - we have to figure it out for ourselves - and so it is with the loss of a child.

I have stumbled along through trial and error. It took me a while to learn the things that help and the things which do not. For instance, it is very easy to fall into a despairing round of dwelling on the awfulness of what has happened, and picking at it endlessly in your mind, but this is so exhausting and unhelpful – though it is fair to say that it is unavoidable at the beginning. In time, I found that exploring new challenges and trying to drive myself forward in a positive way allowed me distraction and distance from my grief, which helps a great deal. With the distance of distraction, it is possible to process grief in a controlled way and at a time of your own choosing.

In 2010, the job that I had held for 11 years came to an end with the retirement of my employer, a hospital consultant, and I found myself with several weeks to fill before I took up a new post within the hospital. The run up to closing the practice was a very stressful time and by the end of it all, I felt as though I had a surfeit of energy to dispel.

I am no athlete, but having previously trained for charity power walking challenges since James died I knew I would benefit from exercise-induced endorphins if I went out walking early in the mornings.

As my exercise regime evolved, I began to observe a significant correlation between that and my grief path and ways in which it has altered with the passage of time.

The summer mornings were warm and still. After a few outings of pounding the streets at a brisk walk, one day I found that what I really wanted to do was to go faster. I picked up pace and broke into a tentative, clumsy, run. I felt terribly conspicuous, as though everyone must be watching me as I passed the houses along the suburban streets, but I carried on. Soon my legs were aching, I was gasping for breath and I needed to stop, but I felt an incredible sense of elation. I had managed to run for only a few minutes, but the point is that I *had* managed to do it. I was reminded of the early days of grief when every breath was torture and I had to keep reminding myself how to do it, when I felt as though I had 'bereaved parent' tattooed onto my forehead and that everyone could see my pain.

As the days went by, I challenged myself in whatever way I could to make myself run a little further. Some days I counted lamp posts. Other days I ran to the length of tracks on my iPod. Gradually I found that I could sustain the pace for longer and longer, without so much effort. And I realised that through running, I could use the world outside, the music on my iPod, my own motion, as a deflector from the relentless thought processes of grief.

This echoed the early stages of loss, of getting from one milestone to the next…so many dates hold special significance when you have lost a child. Each one is tough to approach, but once you have passed it, it recedes slowly behind you into the distance.

My running became a work in progress in the same way as my grieving is a work in progress.

But I now realise that when I first started running, I would find many reasons not to do it properly. I would set off with enthusiasm, then after a few minutes I would slow to a walk/re-tie my laces/change the tracks on my iPod/take some water etc.

It took a while to understand that these were my own 'butterfly mind' tactics to divert me from the matter in hand. For me, there is a definite synergy between running and the grieving process, and these avoidance/diversion techniques can equally be applied to a morning run and traversing the rocky road of grief.

I signed up for a women's Race for Life 5K challenge for the following summer so that I had a six month goal towards which to work.

In the winter months, I retreated from the pavements to the gym and pounded treadmill instead of tarmac, which was somewhat monotonous. It was wonderful to be able to resume running outside when the spring came, just like the gradual emergence from the dark, grey, tedious days of grief I remember, when I could once again notice and take pleasure in the colourful circle of the seasons – that butterfly-like transformation into the way of life that is best described as new normality.

As my stamina increased I found I was more easily achieving the distance targets I set myself, jogging along at an even, comfortable pace without being exhausted afterwards.

What an echo of the evolution of the grief process from the jagged peaks and troughs of the early rollercoaster of emotions into something more measured and calm.
When the day of the Race for Life event dawned I felt excited and nervous but ready for the challenge. I was running for June, a friend who has tackled her recent treatment for breast cancer with remarkable positivity and humour. When I arrived at the venue, my daughter Stella's words of advice were ringing in my ears, "Don't look at everyone's back sign when you are running, mum. You will well up, your throat will tighten and you won't be able to get your breath. Read them before the race, or afterwards."

I didn't really understand what she meant, but I soon saw that each sign pinned to the back of its owner's T shirt told its own story.

That day at Kempton Park, three thousand women ran, jogged or walked the distance for their mums, dads, grandparents, siblings, sons, daughters, stepfamilies, nieces, nephews, uncles, aunts, friends, neighbours, colleagues – indeed, for anyone and everyone affected by cancer.
Seeing this, and knowing that similar Race for Life events are held all around the UK over the summer months was incredibly moving and really brought home to me how many lives are touched by loss.

It is true to say that the ripple effect of loss in a family reaches far beyond those who are immediately involved, expanding beyond the nuclear family to friends, peers, colleagues and the wider community.

Race for Life signifies all that is good about the human spirit - indomitable by nature - to somehow find the strength to reach out to help others in pain and distress.

After Race for Life, I signed up to another event in the autumn, not for sponsorship this time but to try to improve my running time and ensure that I built on the foundations I had laid down with my initial training.

This seems to follow the course of the grieving process, which actually turns out to be a constant in your life. It is always hard work but ultimately it carries reward with the understanding that it is possible to live life post loss in a meaningful and positive way.

On some of my runs, I feel spiritually uplifted, not just physically stretched. Pounding the ground early on a Sunday morning, with no distractions other than having an awareness of my surroundings, I regularly think of James, and I am able to process the emotions surrounding his passing and our resultant loss, with equilibrium. Indeed, it often feels as though he is running in my shadow, encouraging me to push myself that little bit further.

Listening to some of his favourite music tracks on my iPod has enabled me to hear them again without distress. Simply to imagine how he would chuckle at me jogging along to his music is enough to lift my spirits.

Sometimes, too, there will be a feather on the path or a butterfly flitting by that brings James to mind as though he is giving me a nudge.

Our children are still with us, residing within our hearts wherever we go and whatever we are doing. As time passes, it becomes even more important to ensure that their names are spoken and their lives are not forgotten. Our memories of them become ever more precious.

My lesson in grief has certainly turned out to be a need to challenge myself, to keep building my confidence through trying new projects, and to frequently reach a point where I say to myself, "Wow, who would have thought I would be able to do that?" despite what has happened.

My self belief has changed from "Perhaps I can do this" to, "I know I can do this" and that applies equally to my grief path and to running, in fact to all the challenges that I face day to day.

Achievement of any kind is empowering. Empowerment goes a long way towards restoring the confidence that is inevitably shattered following the loss of a child. Given sufficient support and motivation, we are able to rise phoenix-like from our trauma and distress to be stronger than ever. Guidance and help can present themselves in many forms, from formal religious settings to Reiki and other forms of spiritual healing; I believe we are drawn to whatever will help us move forward in our understanding and assimilation of the tragedy and shock of untimely loss. There are many analogies for the grieving process and the other day I was thinking about the miracle of nature that is a hen's egg.

If you hold an egg in front of a candle flame, I am told, you can clearly see the yolk within, tethered at either end but floating free in the safety of its confines.

When James died, my grief resembled a box of eggs dropped on the supermarket floor; in an instant it became a jagged, formless mess. Most people would step round it, not look at it and do their best to pretend it wasn't there. A few people who came close to understanding would help to mop up, but the nursery tale of Humpty Dumpty comes to mind, and it proved impossible to put us all back together again, at least without any cracks.

In the same way as there is a multitude of ways to prepare eggs, there is a multitude of ways to grieve. None is entirely right and none is entirely wrong.

Picture the alchemy of frying an egg - that fascinating transformation from liquid to solid that takes place as an egg white coagulates, whilst the yolk remains soft in the middle. Transformation is a concept that crops up a great deal in grief. The butterfly is one of the best and most common symbols of transformation, reflecting as it does the complete change of one creature to another.

There is nothing in a caterpillar that hints at the promise of a butterfly. Nothing keeps the butterfly held to the ground, but as with an egg yolk, I like to imagine that James' soul is tethered to all those who knew and loved him in this world, but that he also floats free in the afterlife.

Of course, the greatest transformation of an egg is in fertilisation and the ultimate emergence of new life. We emulate this as parents, nurturing our own offspring as they develop and watching over our brood as they form and grow.

Little wonder that the grief of a parent who has lost a nestling prematurely is arguably the deepest, most shocking grief of all.

The most profound human transformation occurs when the soul or spirit leaves the physical body. This is not intended to be a morbid train of thought; rather there is solace to be drawn from witnessing or having an awareness of, the transience of our physical presence.

I was with my dearly loved mum when she died in hospital in 2001 and the actual moment of her passing was deeply awe-inspiring rather than entirely distressing. The split second change from her bodily presence being there...to not being there...was something quite remarkable and I take comfort that I was privileged to witness her passing.

In some way I believe it prepared me to believe and have faith that this profound transformation of the physical to ethereal took place at the moment of James' passing.

In the human condition, regardless of what has befallen us, there is always hope. The American poet Emily Dickinson (1830-1886) says, "Hope is the thing with feathers, that perches in the soul and sings the tune without words, and never stops at all."

More than anything else, I realise that the essence of moving forward is contained in that simple premise; hope.

- Hope of a return to feeling 'normal' again
- Hope that the pain would diminish
- Hope that I would find sufficient peace in my mind to stop questioning why James died so young

- Hope that I would come to appreciate the years we had James with us, rather than dread the future without him

- Hope that I would be able to feel joy again and live my life with purpose and meaning

- Hope that my relationships with family and friends would resume without the awkwardness of grief's presence in the room

- Hope that the lessons from James' passing, once we could see past the grief clearly enough to understand what those lessons were, would enrich those of us who were left behind to live our lives without him

Happily, my hopes have gradually, slowly but surely, been realised. Many elements have contributed to this place of assimilation.

My main drive has been a dogged determination not to let grief and sorrow get the better of me. I cannot over estimate the value of amassing a virtual tool box to help deal with this most traumatic life event. And my experience tells me that the best way is to gather whatever works for you as an individual.

Push yourself to find the energy to take on something that challenges you - and work at it. Achievement is rewarding.

Sometimes it is absolutely necessary for peace of mind to be able to switch off from grieving. At other times, it is possible, even desirable, to meet it head on. These days there is control in my grief so that it has become a place that I visit - in a manner that I choose, and when I choose. Thus the distractions and diversions have lessened over time, as they have done in my running.

Self belief and confidence play great roles in grief recovery. Acceptance of child loss is an alien concept. But assimilation of the event is something that can and does happen over time.

The author Paulo Coelho says, "When faced by any loss there's no point in trying to recover what has been. It's best to take advantage of the large space that opens up before us and fill it with something new."

This is impossible to consider at the beginning of the grieving process. How can anything fill the void that is left by the loss of your child? The answer is that nothing can, but I firmly believe that through sustained hard work, application, concentration and focus one can recover hope for the future and live life with meaning and joy once again.

Grief is tiring! But the renewed hope and optimism that is eventually regained, certainly makes this weariness easier to bear.

I have observed as time goes on that more people are comfortable with mentioning James, than was previously the case. It is as though they feel that sufficient time has elapsed so it is 'safe' to do so. More than one colleague or friend has said that they don't mention him because they don't want to upset me further. My response to this is that I don't ever want James to be forgotten and to hear his name, to talk and laugh about him and his life, is to me a wonderful and very special thing to be able to do. It is lovely to be able to do this with less likelihood of tears than in the early days.

The great British stiff upper lip is not so great when it comes to grief and grieving! We need to be less buttoned up and to say how we really feel. There is no shame in crying with someone in their loss.

But I have learned to make allowances for people who have not encountered traumatic loss, for if I think back to the time before we lost James I would surely not have behaved any differently.

I too would have been one of those people who says helplessly, "I don't know what to say." But I understand better how people feel so useless and shocked in the face of traumatic loss.

It is true to say that there is no manual or textbook that adequately describes, for a bereaved parent or for those counselling a bereaved parent, how to deal with the enormity of bereavement. We do not automatically know how to behave, how to grieve, how to make sense of the turmoil of emotions that comes with this particular form of loss. We must each work through our grief creating our own recipes.

If you take ten people and put them in a kitchen to make a three-egg omelette, the chances are that you will end up with ten different omelettes. So it is with grief. We must all make our own choices and draw on a carefully blended recipe of resources to produce the desired end result; assimilation of loss and hope for the future.

My aim in grieving for my son has from the outset been to do this as positively as possible. The weight of early grief is so massive that it threatens to subsume and swallow one up, but I was determined to come out the other side with a positive and meaningful existence.

I have learned various lessons along the way. Perhaps most importantly, I have gradually moved towards understanding that there is no end point for grief. I relate to the analogy of grief that describes it as a circular staircase. It is indeed like stepping up and stepping down but also stepping round...and round...and round...in never ending fashion.

Elisabeth Kübler-Ross's five-stage grief model (Denial, Anger, Bargaining, Depression and Acceptance) is familiar, and I have often visited it, looking for ways to try to make sense of the process. In fact, the model is actually a misapplication of an original identification of five distinct stages of coping with someone dying. Her research was focused on dying people, who knew they were dying, but this 'one size fits all' model is universally applied for mourning of any type, be it for the loss of a parent, a child or a marriage.

It could be argued that many people have idealised Elisabeth Kübler-Ross's stages; too many people have accepted their linear nature as a standard, even time-limited formula to get them through grief. Laying down a staged grief cycle is formulaic by its nature, but it is difficult to see how else a framework could be devised that would give the newly bereaved an idea of what to anticipate.

Those who know me doubtless appreciate that I was not about to follow any edicts about how and when I should grieve, but that like anyone else flung into the maelstrom of child loss, I was in dire need of some signposts to guide me across a new and totally unfamiliar landscape. Being bereaved is like being told to try to find your way across an alien planet without a map.

Yes, I have experienced all the stages of grief at different times in different ways, and somehow through hard work and application of many resources, I am pleased to affirm that I have arrived at a point of near contentment today.

I recently heard a radio interview with Esther Rantzen, whose long and happy marriage to her husband Desmond Wilcox was well documented. When he died some years ago, she told how she was given a piece of paper by the staff in the Intensive Care Unit, which read, 'These are the stages you will go through: numbness, disbelief, denial, anger, violence...'

Reporting how she felt at the time, she said, "I am sorry, I must have reached violence early."

She went on to say how absurd it is to give anyone rules about grief. This is a view with which I am in accord and although it may be helpful to have a framework for generalisations of the emotions we can reasonably expect, no-one can truly define the path an individual's grief journey will take.

Stage models create expectation of what mourning is meant to be like. I suppose after considering them I allowed myself to expect certain reactions and it was disconcerting when those reactions appeared in the 'wrong' order or not at all. Stages also imply that mourning is passive, which I have certainly found not to be the case.

Think for a moment about a mundane task like cleaning the kitchen. First is the 'sweeping the floor' stage, followed by the 'clean down all the surfaces' stage, followed by the 'bleach stage', and finally the 'drying off and polishing' stage.

The kitchen doesn't do anything but be there, and everything happens to it so that it emerges bright and shiny. No bereaved parent emerges bright and shiny, untouched by his or her experience. We would not be human if we did not experience painful reactions and responses to trauma – but these irrevocably alter how we are for the future.

Grief is rarely, if ever, passive. Rather, especially early on, it is a shouting, roaring, ranting, wailing banshee of a thing which cannot be ignored and has to be squared up to if you are to have any hope of barrelling your way through it. The only time I have found grief to be passive is when it produces a type of exhausted, numb inertia, which I believe is nature's way of giving one a break from relentlessly working the treadmill.

Dr Kübler-Ross does not have the monopoly on staging. Various internet sources suggest that seven stage grief models may be applied. However, these should be viewed with a degree of caution, since such models are based on observations of select populations, which are not necessarily subject to evidence-based scientific study. A grief model which I read about in an article on the Yahoo! Contributor Network suggests this sixth stage, more or less as an add-on to the Kübler-Ross stages:

"Testing and Reconstruction. The hallmark of this stage is an attempt to solve the practical problems posed by the loss. A person in this stage may begin to engage in normal life activities again, may evaluate financial obligations or living arrangements, and may begin reaching out more to other people."

I like the positive message in this stage which represents a place I reached at around the four-year mark. This was the time when I began to socialise again and pick up some friendships that were much neglected. This was the time that I was able to feel more 'normal' again, albeit a new 'normal'. The old me is gone forever and those around me have had to take their own time getting to know the new me.

I too have had to take time to get to know the new me! The loss of the self I knew was a shock. For 49 years, I knew myself well and I disappeared overnight. It has taken a while to come to terms with an irreversibly altered persona.

American Mitch Carmody writes prolifically on grief since the loss of his son Kelly in 1987 and he too challenges Elisabeth Kübler-Ross. Since the loss of his son, Mitch has dedicated his life to serving the bereaved through his writing, art, an active online forum resource and various workshops in the US.

Mitch has produced his own grief model that he calls 'the S.T.A.I.R.S model. which I replicate with his permission.

"I believe there are no predictable linear stages in processing the death of a loved one. Although widely accepted for many years I do not think the five stages of grief as proposed by Elisabeth Kübler-Ross adequately represent the true journey for most of the bereaved. I believe it is a series of steps negotiated one at a time, each one taking as long as it takes to reach the next; no timetable; no shortcuts; no false expectations; no failures; just one step at a time; climbing the S.T.A.I.R.S. when we are ready, willing, and able. Each step takes as long as it takes and is different for everyone. Whether it is a long-term illness that took our loved one's life, a sudden unexpected accident, murder or suicide, it is we who are left behind who will have to climb this stairway.

I experienced sudden death when my twin sister and her two boys were killed in an auto accident and I was propelled into instant shock and grief. Shortly after their deaths, my son was diagnosed with cancer, which we battled hard for two years. I witnessed him endure a lot of pain much of that time, but I never stopped praying for a miracle. We did receive a miracle but unfortunately it was not a cure. I accepted the fact he was going to die, but that did not prepare me for his death.

When Kelly died I was swept into shock and grief again. Anticipatory grief I believe is a myth, there is no such thing. When we maintain hope, we never accept or prepare for death when it strikes. We cannot anticipate the pain of separation no matter how it happens. Sudden death and long-term illness are two side roads that merge onto the same main road of survival to accept the unacceptable. You love hard, you grieve hard; your intensity of grief is directly proportionate to the depth of your love, your own grief is the hardest to bear.

Grief is complex and unyielding and if not dealt with in some proactive manner can lead to post traumatic stress syndrome many years down the road.

Active participation in our grief journey is paramount to survival. If we want to feel good again, feel joy again, feel part of the world again, we should strive to become an *intentional survivor* and not a hapless victim. Seek help, read, and journal, reach out to others in pain, set a goal no matter how small, grieve out of the box, mourn and lament without shame. Live your loss. Ascend those stairs knowing that you must do so to survive, but also realise gravity increases dramatically during the grieving process...so take it slow, baby steps.

S.T.A.I.R.S.

The 1st step is *Shock*. Our loved one dies; we are in reactionary disbelief and we are numb head to *soul*. This is how we are able to choose a casket, sign papers, read sympathy cards and publicly share our grief with so many. We are in a primal stage of survival, we function as an automaton and we accomplish the impossible: We bury or cremate the body of our loved one.

The 2nd step is *Trauma*. This is the ensuing reality of our loss and our struggle to comprehend it and weave it into the fabric that is our daily life. This may be the step where the bereaved linger the longest. When we return to work, by rote go through the holidays and struggle everyday to cope. Every morning when we open our eyes after our fitful night's sleep and we again sword fight with denial and disbelief. The light of a new day beckons us to rejoin the world that we are reticent to embrace. Moving forward, functioning at all seems we are dishonouring our loved one. We know there is no going back; we do not want to move forward so we stay where we are for as long as it takes.

The 3rd step is *Acceptance/Assimilation*. This is the most powerful step in moving forward in processing our loss; when we accept the loss has taken place we can then make plans for the future as nebulous as it may seem; this is not an easy admission to make but a crucial one for our survival. Accepting the reality of the loss is not forgetting or letting go, its living with the loss and accepting its collateral damage to our future.

The 4th step is *Introspection/Insight*. This is where we look deep within ourselves to try and find ourselves. We question our faith and seek to find the 'meaning of life' in the depths of our sorrow.

We use the tools of intuition, gut feelings and prayer to access the world inside and out in a different light of perception.

The more we know, the more we know what we don't know. We look to find answers to the whys and the cries of our wounded soul ... and are finally willing to hear the answers.

The 5th step is *Reinvestment/Rebuilding/Renaissance*. This is where we take charge of our journey and find creative ways, and healthy ways, to process our loss. This is what I call 'Proactive Grieving' where in earnest we attempt to reconstruct the foundation of a life that has been shattered and try to regain the joy back which is our birthright. We become Intentional Survivors. This is where we can make a difference in the world and fulfil our personal destiny. When we honour our loved one's life by creating a legacy in their name the world is then enriched instead of diminished.

The 6th step is *Serenity and true peace*. This is not always possible in this world, loss or no loss in our lives, but yet it is attainable. It may take years, even decades to reach or it creeps into our lives on the journey itself...when we are caught by surprise to see the face in the mirror is smiling. Miracles do happen...believe."

Another aspect of grief that jumped up at me early on was fear. I remember that at first, I was deeply afraid of becoming overcome, engulfed and embittered by grief from my loss.

The author C S Lewis expresses this very well in "A Grief Observed": "No-one ever told me that grief felt so like fear. I am not afraid, but the sensation is like being afraid. The same fluttering in the stomach, the same restlessness, the yawning. I keep on swallowing.

At other times it feels like being mildly drunk, or concussed. There is a sort of invisible blanket between the world and me. I find it hard to take in what anyone says. Or perhaps, hard to want to take it in. It is so uninteresting. Yet I want the others to be about me. I dread the moments when the house is empty. If only they would talk to one another and not to me."

My way of countering this helpless fear was to take on a variety of challenges, confronting those crises which threatened to overwhelm me.

I discovered that focusing on new activities, from spiritual practice to walking, running and cycling, all have an uplifting and positive effect.

I discovered displacement tactics to cope and move forward another small step on the journey at times when my mind threatened to get stuck in grief.

I discovered that expressing grief in writing is a powerful and cathartic tool. It is especially useful to look back over what I have written as a measure of progress.

I discovered the need to be introspective and visit my grief quietly and sit with it when I have to, or conversely to have a good angry rant at the Fates. Both reactions are helpful.

I feel that I have been slow in fully realising quite how immeasurable is the impact of our loss on my husband, daughter and stepchildren, and I will always feel immense regret that that we and the wider family do not have the same unhampered continuance of life experienced by the non-bereaved family. When a child dies, there are no new memories or future events to share and anticipate in relation to that child, and this emphasises the difference between families who are living through child loss and those who are not.

Grief unavoidably carries a measure of guilt, with which the bereft have to learn to live. Family events such as birthdays, Christmas, weddings, the arrival of grandchildren, all serve to emphasise the absence of the loved one who should be here to share our joys. It is difficult to resist the 'what if' game where one can create scenarios in which you and/or the lost child did something different, resulting in the child still being alive. The guilt that as a parent you should have been able to prevent what happened to your child descends like a fog and it is very slow to dissipate.

As the guilt over the loss diminishes it may be replaced by a different guilt - that you can begin to enjoy your life again with a return to optimism and anticipation of pleasurable events, such as holidays.

I firmly believe bereaved parents should allow themselves to feel happy again, without any guilt, if they are able.

"Don't walk in front of me, I may not follow. Don't walk behind me, I may not lead. Walk beside me and be my friend." (Albert Camus).

My father told me many years ago that by the time you reach adulthood, you can count your true friends on the fingers of one hand.

The loss of a child has a huge effect on friendship. Some friendships are seemingly unaltered, whilst others can never go back to the way they were before (much like we ourselves cannot).

Looking back over a period of time I can see that my relationships with friends and acquaintances have changed, not only because of my profound grief which caused them discomfort, but because of my evolution into the person I have become since my loss. I am now that same-but-different person. And whilst some people can adapt quite happily to the new me, other friends simply cannot cope with that. For my part, it has taken a while for me not to feel betrayed by those friends who, by unstated mutual agreement, have gradually drifted out of my life.

Being a friend to someone who is grieving requires greater than usual attention to the needs of the friendship in order for it to remain strong and to grow stronger. My friends have learned to take cues from me, to know when I feel keen to talk about my loss, and when I would rather not. My friends are not judgmental and allow me to say what I need without trying to diminish or dilute the strength of the feelings that I express.

I understand that my friends cannot imagine what I am going through. But they know me well enough to realise that they don't need to keep telling me that! I know they cannot comprehend my loss, but if I'm unable to offload my feelings and emotions onto my friends, who can I offload them to? I would add at this point that my family members are counted in with my friends.

Some people try to relate to loss when their children have 'near misses' in their lives. One friend told me how she understood how I felt because her son was involved in an accident and 'could have been killed'. She caught me at a bad moment. "How dare she say she understands how I feel because she *nearly* lost her son?" I ranted and railed. "Nearly is not the same. Nearly does not mean she has to adjust to life without him, does it?! He is still alive, still here with everyone just like before!"

With the passage of time I was able to take a slightly less jaundiced view as I came to understand that she truly believed that the 'near-miss' gave her some insight to how I feel. But of course it is not the same. Her son is still living, after all.

I don't want to name those friends who are really there for me, as opposed to those who are not. That would be grossly unfair and could further damage the fragility of the friendships that have been adversely affected, which still manage to cling on because of other aspects of shared past. Friendships are not all about grieving. They can be work-based friendships or friendships made in the maternity unit when our babies are born, or those rather special friendships with women the same age, whose children are the same age. We follow our course as mothers through all the phases of childhood – exchanging the ups and downs of the day-to-day life of parents, juggling our jobs, after school activities and family relationships. As women, our friendships are deep and complex and encompass a wide range of emotions surrounding our families.

I have both gained and lost friendships through grief. I have made new friendships with bereaved parents and I have made new friendships with non-bereaved parents.

Each friendship contributes another small segment to the vast jigsaw puzzle that represents the ongoing grief journey. Some of my friendships are entirely virtual. I reached out in the online bereavement forums of TCF and DSN very early in my loss, desperate to find other bereaved mothers and sometimes, an inexplicable connection happens with someone who responds but whom you may never meet. You exchange emails about your children for a time. You may divulge some very personal information and yet it does not feel wrong or strange to do so. There is an implicit trust as you recognise in each other a need to confide.

Some of these friendships endure, some of them fizzle out because they have served their purpose. They remind me of the much circulated and shared Reason, Season, Lifetime poem:

People come into your life for a reason, a season or a
lifetime.
When you figure out which one it is,
you will know what to do for each person.

When someone is in your life for a REASON,
it is usually to meet a need you have expressed.
They have come to assist you through a difficulty;
to provide you with guidance and support;
to aid you physically, emotionally or spiritually.
They may seem like a godsend, and they are.
They are there for the reason you need them to be.
Then, without any wrongdoing on your part or at an
inconvenient time,
this person will say or do something to bring the
relationship to an end.
Sometimes they die. Sometimes they walk away.
Sometimes they act up and force you to take a stand.

What we must realise is that our need has been met, our desire fulfilled; their work is done.
The prayer you sent up has been answered and now it is time to move on.
Some people come into your life for a SEASON, because your turn has come to share, grow or learn.
They bring you an experience of peace or make you laugh.
They may teach you something you have never done.
They usually give you an unbelievable amount of joy.
Believe it. It is real. But only for a season.
LIFETIME relationships teach you lifetime lessons; things you must build upon in order to have a solid emotional foundation.
Your job is to accept the lesson, love the person, and put what you have learned to use in all other relationships and areas of your life.
It is said that love is blind but friendship is clairvoyant.

Of the friendships that I have made through TCF, there is a group of four of us who have formed our own mutual support group. We meet regularly – perhaps half a dozen times a year – and we have done so since initially making contact through the TCF online forum in 2006. We almost invariably meet at the same pub on Saturday lunchtime, and we eat, talk, laugh and cry together. The dynamics of our group are such that we relate to each other in a deeply personal way – of course – because we all have that one dreadful thing in common, the loss of our child; that is the glue that binds us. We have lost sons of differing ages in varying circumstances and we each have totally diverse grief experiences. By sharing our journeys with one another in a safe and sociable environment, we have given each other much comfort, hope and strength over the years.

I am protecting the anonymity of our group and the personal nature of the confidences of our friendship, but the following themes and observations result from our many meetings.

When we are together, we laugh a lot. This may sound strange, but our humour is something that we need; the release of laughter to expunge some of the worst of the grief from our systems. To be able to do this in a safe and familiar environment is worth a huge amount to all of us. Equally, if one of us is having a bit of a wobbly day, we can provide support in the way that we have all learned in the evolution of our friendship. We understand the need to put on a mask to the outside world to hide our grief, but when we are together, we don't have to be strong for anyone else and we can reveal our true feelings without concern.

We often talk about how our friendship works and what it gives us, individually and collectively. It is undoubtedly valuable because there are no limits. We can talk about anything we wish, but it is fair to say that people who have not experienced our type of loss, would not understand some of our conversations and reactions at all. Our sense of humour is somewhat dark!

Sometimes, particularly in the early days, it felt as though we were trying to outdo each other in relating the unwittingly stupid comments that people made to us. This undoubtedly helped us to process our early emotions into a slightly more tolerant place...eventually. Our early outrage has decreased to greater tolerance, most of the time.

I believe our friendship is cathartic for all of us. When we have the need, we can express our frustrations in a way that we could not do elsewhere. For example, if we meet in the run up to Christmas we can exchange – and laugh about – things that are said to us, such as workmates or friends asking us if we are looking forward to the festive season. As time has passed, we have all gained a better understanding of how little the non-bereaved are able to comprehend about the way we live our lives. We live with the presence of our grief that does not leave us for a second and each of us recognises this in the other.

People have short memories and we can cut them more slack now than we did in the early days. But it certainly helps for us to be able to express resentment or annoyance among people who really understand and do not judge in any way, and this is one of the most valuable aspects of our friendship.

We talk about the impact of our loss on our partners and our families and all recognise the ripple effect on all our relationships. Sadly, it is all too normal for some family connections to be irrevocably fragmented by the loss. We all have longstanding friendships that have been permanently altered by our loss. We have discussed friends who couldn't cope because what had happened was 'too close to their safe little world.' We have experienced the feeling of being treated as if we could be contagious and as if that something sad or bad will happen to friends who communicate with us.

When we socialise now, we all find it can be difficult to be with new people. The unasked questions about children and families sit like the 'elephant in the room' for us in many social situations. We all find we manipulate conversations to avoid talking about what happened so as not to upset anyone – and this protection of other people's feelings is definitely something that happens later in grief. It becomes easier to be selective about who to tell and who not to tell.

As time passes, we all recognise too the altered nature of our ongoing friendships. There is tremendous value in our being able to air issues with each other that have cropped up since our loss, and to get advice from each other on how to deal with these new experiences. One of us resents those she calls 'nibbling people' – those people who want to know what happened to her son and keep on asking her until she is forced to tell them, when she would not necessarily have chosen to.

All four of us have variable amounts of time when we are able to grieve, due to our various commitments. Whereas I find release in writing, another might need to have the occasional duvet day, or produce artwork. We grieve entirely differently, yet we all feel we are slowly and inexorably moving along the healing path that is right for us. It is difficult to pinpoint how we learn the things that are right and the things that are wrong, but somehow we manage it. By sharing our individual experiences, collectively we have evidence that we are getting it right in our own fashion. That is an invaluable outcome of our friendship.

We enjoy the fact that we can 'flow between talking about the depths of our despair and move on to the fun stuff.' More recently, we have all shared much of our everyday lives, what's going on within our families and so on, rather than our lunches merely focusing on our grief and loss as they did in the early days.

I expect that these days, we appear to others like any other group of four women meeting for lunch and a catch up. But we ourselves know we are not simply 'ladies who do lunch.'

Our regular meetings are proof, if it were needed, that this friendship was destined to evolve into the cohesive unit it has become from our first meeting, when we tentatively began to share the intimacies of our losses. We reached out to one another in a very unique way, and the value of each and every one of our meetings is inestimable. We are a true representation of Compassionate Friends.

We can see just how far we have come, and we are agreed that our lives are like a tapestry or a piece of knitting. Holes appeared in it when we lost our sons. Over time, the holes are being darned back together, but we can never restore the perfection of the original article, without the presence of our dear boys. All four of us keep alive our precious memories by sharing our experiences and telling the stories of our precious sons; and there is no doubt we help each other immensely along our never-ending journey. There does not need to be any end point to our meetings; they are so valuable for all of us that they will doubtless continue for many years to come.

New friendships made in adulthood are to be savoured as something fresh and special in our lives and they seem particularly precious after bereavement, whether or not loss is the instigating factor in the friendship. I enjoy sharing stories of James with friends who never met him, even though they cannot know him. Through trying to cherish every friendship for what it means to me at the time, it becomes easier to accept the few friends who appeared to abandon me when I needed them.

Some friendships are withdrawn because people are afraid to share their children's progress and achievements after you have lost your child. This is so sad. It is done with the best of intentions so as not to 'upset' us, but one of the main points that is missed by the non-bereaved is this simple fact; we cannot be any more saddened than we already are. The worst thing that could happen to us as parents has happened to us.

Therefore, if you want to tell me that your son or daughter has just been awarded an Olympic medal or secured that dream job in New York, please rest assured this news will not upset me any further. Indeed, I like to hear of the achievements of my friends' offspring and share in their joy. It is uplifting rather than disheartening. Of course, I have wistful moments of wishing that it could be James getting the gong, but deep down I am delighted - on a good day, anyway.

It is a fact that not everyone who was your friend before your child's passing will be your friend during and after your grief and mourning.

But the loss is not entirely yours because those friends who drift away then miss the opportunity to see that you are able to grow and flourish, not only in spite of, but because of, what has befallen you.

And they may be missing the chance to have an even better friend in you, in the future.

If you are wondering what it takes to be a friend to a grieving parent, or indeed to a person who is grieving for any other loss - because grief is universal after all - the following are good pointers:

- A friend to a person in grief is someone they can confide in and trust implicitly

- A friend does not judge or analyse the views of the grieving person or try to change them. Listening and empathising is the most important skill here

- A friend is willing to listen, sometimes just share silence with the grieving person, and accept their tears

- A friend encourages the grieving person to share their memories and never to be afraid to speak the name of their loved one

- Finally, I include this quote attributed to Charles Caleb Colton, "A real friend is one who walks in when the rest of the world walks out."

Genuine friends during your grief are willing to walk beside you during the darkest moments of your sorrow, supporting you whilst at the same time knowing that this is 'your stuff', not 'their stuff' and they can offer you their strength whilst remaining buffered against your weaknesses.

These are the friends who, instead of saying "Let me know what I can do", call you regularly or turn up on your doorstep, ready to be there for you in whatever capacity you need them.

Through simply being there for you, the genuine friends encourage all the small steps and milestones that mark your progress in your grief experience. They smile with you, listen to you, laugh with you, and cry with you.
Where would we be without them?

Signs

Lost to us, but never gone
Their young spirits party on
(can you hear his joyful laugh
When you find a feather on the path?
Who made the rainbow that gave you joy?
It must have been that thoughtful boy)
They are in our shadows as we tread each mile
They make us weep, but also smile
I'm sure they watch us with love and pride
Admiring how we cope with the rocky ride
Our boys are bound up with so much love
Surely we can feel it from beyond and above
See them in the days, dream them in the night
Feel them in the breeze and dawn's soft light
Watch them in the clouds scudding by
Sense their presence in the clear blue sky
Remember them in manhood and as young boys
Be comforted always by their lifetime of joys.

Andrea Corrie, 2007

Chapter 9

Grieving in The Now

"You may not control all the events that happen to you, but you can decide not to be reduced by them."

Maya Angelou

The time frame for my personal journey through grief is impossible to set down. It is only in looking back year on year that I can evaluate moving along to the point where I am now.

The point where I am now is different from the point where I was this time last year, and different again from the point I will be at this time next year.

Thank goodness for the evolution! For if we did not move forwards or progress, we would land up mired in a spiral of hopelessness.

Does grief make a better person of you? I think it both humbles and enlightens, even ultimately enriches with understanding. These days my perception of others is a gentler thing. I may be more tolerant than I used to be, though I find I have little patience for trivial complaints in others. Everyone has grief, trauma, strife. We do not all wear it all the time. But to extend your feelings of empathy to those who are simply unable to understand what you are going through, because they themselves are fortunate enough not to have similar experience, is a tough thing to do in the beginning. It is easy to see others' lives as blessed when you are struggling with the trauma of loss.

It is easy to be impatient with those who don't know what to say to you – but you come to realise that you too would have been the same before your loss.

Certainly I think grief can give you strengths you did not know you possessed, and finding the fortitude to cope with grief leads you to tackle that which you hitherto thought impossible. When you think about it, once you have been faced with the loss of your child, nothing that is thrown at you in life can ever hold the same level of gut-wrenching fear.

I have the greatest admiration for my dear friend Karen in Melbourne. We met online through DSN. Karen has lifelong claustrophobia and fear of flying but she has conquered it since her son Sam died. She has managed a couple of flights within Australia and she and her husband are planning a trip to the UK. We cannot wait to meet them.

It is often said that after child loss, your address book changes, and I would agree. My post loss friends, those whom I have met through the Drowning Support Network and the Compassionate Friends, are particularly important. Our friendships have evolved from the initial focus of our grief into more typical rounded friendships. But, there is an incalculable value in being able to call upon others who truly understand what it is like to be a bereaved parent. Also, pre loss friends may see you as untouchable or unreachable. They wait for you to return to your 'old self' and sometimes cannot cope with the disappearance of that self.

I have also made some new friends entirely unrelated to bereavement, which feels like healthy progress. Early on in grief, loss colours everything and I would not have been able to focus on new relationships with others.

During my writing research, especially more recently, I have been intrigued to note the amount of grief writing that is accessible online. When I first started writing in 2005, it seems to me that there were fewer people publicly expressing their emotions in the written word. But if I type 'grief writing after child loss' into a Google search box today, it immediately brings up a raft of worldwide material.

Writing is cathartic. It helps to create a sense of order from your thoughts, even if at the beginning the mind is totally chaotic. Stella recently came across some letters I had written to her in the first few years after James died. She said, "I don't know how you did it mum; your thought processes on paper were so clear even though you were in such turmoil."

She went on to say, "It's funny really, the first few letters look as though they were scrawled with little planning, but later on your writing is neater and it is obvious you took time over what you were saying."

As Stella lives over 200 miles away in Cornwall, I often write to her – we are in touch by phone and email but sometimes there is no substitute for a heartfelt letter, and I am glad she was able to see progress in my writing.

In 2010, I joined a creative writing group called 'writing from experience' and this not only gave me some respite from grief writing, in that we were encouraged to write light fiction, but it also helped me a great deal in structuring writing correctly.

But for any grieving parent, whether or not they can write, putting thoughts down on paper is never anything other than helpful. I have written poems to James, and letters that he will never read, but the act of creating a piece of writing brings its own satisfaction.

There follows a favourite quote, originally published by the Compassionate Friends, which reached me via my friend Sandra. She channels grief for the loss of her son into artistic works of painting and sculpture, which give colourful voice to her sorrow. Sandra is an admirable example of how expressing grief creatively and sharing the results with others can be an effective tool in the armoury of the mourning journey.

"I am not alone and you are not alone. For as surely as the intangible things you left behind are with me, so a part of me stepped quietly with you, across the threshold of tomorrow. And as the brilliance of a star, in a dark sky, so in my heart is a memory of you – endless, beautiful, indestructible."

Such beautiful, thought provoking words – and Sandra has incorporated this quote into a piece of artwork thus creating a dual form of expression.

I have learned to formulate ways to cope and to move forward in living a meaningful and positive life through utilising whatever means I can put at my disposal to help me get by.

Yes, I can now lay down new memories to take me forward but at the same time I balance them with the memories of the son I have lost; thoughts of the future he should have had are never far from my mind.

Last year, my husband Shaun and I felt that the time was right to contemplate downsizing from our family home and with the usual attendant stress of property transactions, we moved house. We have moved a short distance - only eight miles - and we are settling well into our new environment. Of course we had anxieties about leaving James behind. However, a friend said, "Don't worry. You will pack up your memories of James along with your boxes. When new people come into your house they don't see your memories. They don't see your events, happy or sad. They bring in their own with them."

This made me feel much better about being somewhere that James has not lived with us. It would have been very different early in our grief. Perhaps it works for some people who must break ties to achieve a modicum of peace, but I know that had we moved earlier, which was a temptation at one point, it would merely have been an attempt to run away from the pain.

The day we moved into our new home, I put my favourite photos of James in a place where we see them every day, and I have faith that he is here with us, in spirit.

Our new, more rural, location is a source of great joy to me; we are close to the Basingstoke canal and I am getting to know it through walking, running and cycling. To experience the beauty of the changing seasons, to see the wildlife and enjoy the colours of nature in all her splendour is wonderful; truly it is like healing balm to the soul.

I feel something of James in all my outings in the area and I often recall the following epitaph, written for a young soldier who lost his life in Afghanistan.

"Listen for him, in the rustling of the branches, and the rippling of the stream."

Even though this is a place where James has not lived, I feel his presence in the beauty of the surroundings and I am able to revisit thoughts of my loss with a gentle sorrow, rather than the desperate longing that marked the early days of grief.

In fact, it has come as quite a surprise to me how easily I have accepted living in a place where there is no history of James. Our previous house was naturally full of memories of him, and I will admit that it is easier for me to live somewhere that I am not constantly reminded of both his presence and his absence. Moving house after loss is a conundrum for many and I was anxious about it beforehand, but I have been reassured by my level of contentment. I am not sure that I would have been so sanguine about it had we moved earlier on.

In time, through bits and pieces of assimilation of our loss, we see that we cannot maintain the past intact. It has been forever changed and we must readjust. It is a hard task but not unachievable. This is my loss; this is the hand I have been dealt and it is up to me to play it as best I am able for the sake of my son and all who know me.

Some people turn to their faith to support and sustain them through grief. This is not an avenue that I chose to follow, but I have found a great deal of help in exploring different complementary therapies and belief systems, such as spiritual healing and energy healing such as Reiki.

The holistic approach towards mind, body and spirit holds appeal and it certainly does nobody any harm to explore their psyche and how the mental and physical body can work together in healing ways.

It is interesting as I have come to know various healers who, more often than not, have come to healing through trauma and loss of their own. It takes a special type of person to be able to reach out and help others in their time of need, and for me it doesn't matter whether this is through prayer, laying on of hands, or lighting candles. All healing therapy is good healing therapy in my book.

The anniversary date is always testing. When I look back over each year since 2006, it is really difficult to distinguish one from another. Perhaps this is because we observe certain rituals that have become an important part of the day, and because we follow a similar agenda each time, no single anniversary stands out from the other years.

We did, however, do one thing differently this year. Last year, we visited the crematorium in the morning and went to Kingston on the same day, and I found the emotional toll of that was too great. This is just a personal thing, but I like to go to the crem when there is no-one else around and as it is close to where we now live, I can choose to go early, on my way to work.

Shaun gives me free rein to plan the anniversary day. He says that he is happy – if that is the right word – to go along with anything I want to do.

The only way to recall with any clarity the progression of a day is to record it as it happens, which I did on the eighth anniversary, Sunday 28 July 2013:

7.00am: I'm wide awake but it is far too early to get up on a Sunday morning. I lie in the quiet stillness and think of the day ahead. Shaun is peacefully asleep and I lean into his back and close my eyes for another little doze.

7.40am: Minstrel the cat decides it is time for me to get up and make a cup of tea. He peers earnestly into my face and a puff of his fishy breath is enough to push me out of bed. I go through the autopilot morning tasks of making the tea and decide I will go for a run, so as well as Shaun's cup of tea I fix myself a strong shot of coffee with sugar to boost my energy levels.

8.00am: I have popped back to bed for ten minutes to have a cuddle and a quick chat with Shaun. We ask each other how we slept and then, "Going for a run, dear?" he asks me, knowing the fact that I have made myself coffee rather than tea confirms my intention.

"Yes," I say. "I can have a think about the day and then come back, have a shower and some breakfast before we go to Kingston."

Shaun asks me how I am feeling and I ask him how he is feeling. We agree we are both feeling all right so far and I get ready to go out for my run.

I check my phone before I go. There are already texts and Facebook messages for us from family, our friends and James' friends. How heartwarming it is to have this support.

As the years pass it would be easy to think other people forget, but they do not.

8.20am: I set off with my iPod playing a selection of my and James' favourite tunes. I think about him constantly as I jog along in the early morning calm. It is sunny and warm and I am soon into a comfortable pace as I run alongside the Basingstoke canal, marvelling at the tranquillity of the surroundings. The trees are lush and green and the birds out-sing my iPod.

It is strange, I muse, that James lost his life to water and yet…I find this environment so very healing. I have not been put off water, be it river, stream, lake, pond, canal or ocean, by what happened to him. Water was a natural environment to James throughout his lifetime. He was a good, strong swimmer which makes it all the more poignant that he lost his life to water, but perhaps I should draw comfort that he died in what was for him, an elemental and familiar environment. Maybe he was not shocked, maybe he found it an easy passing. We can never know, but I like to think so.

9.00am: I reach my halfway point, the bridge and lock that is two miles or so from home. Here I stop to catch my breath. I find tears on my cheeks and allow myself the indulgence of weeping, here in the Sunday morning serenity, where no-one can see me. One of James' much loved songs is playing – the Carpenters 'On top of the World' – inappropriate perhaps, but it makes me smile through my tears.

9.20am: I am back home and feel exhilarated by my run, as usual, if rather hot and in need of a shower!

Shaun is dressed and ready and also as usual, he has to wait for me to undergo my normal cleansing and grooming preparations. What a good job he is such a patient man! Although today, he says, 'I really can't wait to get on our way. It feels like a long morning.'

10.20am: Another hour has passed and we are breakfasted and ready to set off.

We bought the flowers to place at James' plaque yesterday – I like to get sunflowers or some other bright blooms and it seemed good synchronicity to find just one bunch of eight sunflowers available. I always tuck a small handwritten card in amongst the flowers – I composed this in my mind whilst out on my run, and it didn't take long for me to write it. This time I used a postcard – a picture from a painting by the artist Pierre Bonnard. This seemed fitting as I took Stella and James to an exhibition of his paintings at the Tate Gallery years ago. We occasionally enjoyed a 'cultural day out' in London and I think the children humoured me on these days if they were bored, but we always had something of an adventure on such outings. They left me with fond memories.

On our drive to Kingston, Shaun and I talked about our feelings. I asked him how he feels he has processed his grief over the years. He said, "When I am working, particularly when I am out on my own doing mindless tasks that I have done a million times before…then I can let my mind wander and think about things, and process my memories and my thoughts."

There is a whole raft of things that could be said about the different ways in which women and men grieve and process their grief.

This admission from Shaun was about as much information as he ever gives and I think it is a typical male response – if there is such a thing. He does not appear to need to talk to anyone else about his grief – apart from to me – and it has taken me a while to accept that this is his way of doing things and if it were wrong for him, I figure I would know by now.

I also think it is fair to suppose that step parents grieve differently from parents. I am not saying their loss is any more difficult or any easier to bear, but it may be different because there is not the blood tie, however long the step family has existed. I have suggested to Shaun before that he has not only grief for James to contend with, but also, because James died a scant six weeks after we were married, he has had to accept that our newlywed future was rocked to its foundations. Not an easy thing to take on.

For myself, I know that writing plays a great part in processing my emotions, but there is also a place for the different activities I have taken up since James died – from spiritual practice to running – which are all a form of distraction. By this I mean that whilst I am doing these other things, there is a part of my mind that can run free and visit my grief in a controlled and comfortable way. Perhaps it is not so very different from Shaun's way, after all.

11.00am: We arrive in Kingston and park opposite the police station. I always feel uncomfortable passing the police station as it takes me back to the interview we had with the detective inspector who was in charge of James' case. Our police liaison officers took us there soon after James had been found, so that we could discuss the police investigation, the progress that had been made, and so on.

I can remember how unreal it felt at the time to sit in his cramped office listening to his unemotional recounting of the facts.

We also pass the council offices, where our campaign to institute safety measures at the riverside was dealt with, and this brings back a multitude of memories too. I worked in an office in that very building many years ago. What a strange twist of fate it was to be brought back to that place again.

However, it is time to take a deep breath and focus on the current time, not the past. It is easy to look back to what is known, harder to look forward into the unknown.

11.15am: We leave the main road and walk along the pedestrianised riverside area towards Kingston bridge. All around us are restaurants and leisure facilities. The area is popular and on a sunny day like today, there are many people around; families, the young and elderly, tourists, students and locals – a real cosmopolitan mix that reflects the society of a university town like Kingston.
Shaun and I hold hands, and I notice our hands are getting clammy.

As we approach the area where the plaque is placed, alongside the steps leading to the water, I am aware of my quickening heartbeat and a feeling of anxiety, though I couldn't say why. As we get closer to the plaque area we can see that there is no-one sitting on the steps there (as there sometimes is).

"Good," I say to Shaun. "There's no-one there." He nods in agreement before going down the steps to loop the bunch of sunflowers through the metal boat ring set against the wall.

To make sure the flowers do not fall out, and are not interfered with in any way, Shaun wraps a piece of wire around them. I take a few photos with the camera on my phone. I always feel a need to record events, whether or not I share them afterwards via social media. Today, though, I knew I would share an image on Facebook later. We stand at the top of the steps for a few minutes, leaning on the railings, lost in our own thoughts. Suddenly I hear a woman's voice reading out the wording on the plaque: "In loving memory of James Edward Clark....,"she reads and then exclaims, "Oh, look, there are flowers there."

As she looks more closely she realises the date on the plaque.

I cannot help myself.

"He was my son," I say. "It's eight years ago today. That's why we are here."

The poor woman didn't know what to say or do. She and the girl she was reading to, probably her daughter, with perhaps a boyfriend or partner – just looked at me, stricken. Shaun put his arm around me and we walked away towards the bridge, in horribly awkward embarrassment.

I felt bad for saying anything, but I really couldn't stop myself. It was one of the moments that bereaved parents become used to, when there is a split second decision to be made – do I say something, or don't I? I really cannot say if I got it right this time.

11.30am: We walked along to the bridge and noticed changes this year from previous years.

"Look," said Shaun, pointing to some hoardings running behind the trees at the back of the towpath. "It looks as though there is some development happening here."

We both realised at the same time that proposed restaurant names were listed on the hoardings and, we were pleased to see that the nightclub where James spent his last evening was also behind the hoarding and will presumably become a restaurant when the nightclub licence expires in 2019.

Thank goodness it looks as though the nightclub will be no more, for we found it impossible to believe that planning permission had originally been granted for a late night venue so close to the water. We are sure that the more stringent rules of today would now preclude such a decision.

11.45am: We walked back to the plaque again and stood for a few more moments. The woman who read the plaque was still there and she moved away, I like to think that was out of respect but perhaps she felt embarrassed. If I had the opportunity I would have liked to have told her more about what happened to James, but it was obvious that she did not wish to be approached.

12.00am: We walked away from the area with relief. The knot in my stomach loosened and Shaun said he felt exactly the same. The first and most important part of our ritual had been observed.

"What's it to be, then?" he asked me as we walked along. "Cornish Pasty or Sausage Roll?"

Somehow we were both suddenly very hungry and only something calorific and naughty would do! We agreed on sausage rolls and a cold drink and took them to a relatively peaceful garden area to eat them. I say 'relatively' because we chose the old Memorial Gardens which, today, had a strange atmosphere to them. This had less to do with the deceased occupants of the graves – which are very old – and more to do with the unfortunate, rather loud drunks who frequent the area. So we did not spend as long there as we would have wished and it was not particularly relaxing. 12.30pm: Retail therapy needs to figure in our anniversary day and Kingston is one of the best shopping centres outside of London.

I have reined myself in a bit, to say the least. On the first anniversary in 2006 I took it into my head to change my car; went to the local Seat garage, did a test drive on a nearly new vehicle and traded in my own that day. Impulsive? – Yes indeed, but I think I needed the diversion at the time to deflect me from the awfulness of the anniversary itself.

So, back to 2013. We went to Marks and Spencer and I bought a pretty, brightly coloured top to cheer my mood. Then I said to Shaun, "You know, I haven't got a decent candle to light for James this evening. Let's go and find one."

We looked here and there and eventually I found a scented candle in a glass that we both liked. But as we walked through the home department of M and S, I spied a lovely glass candle stand, large enough to take a pillar candle.

"Oh, I must have one of those!" I exclaimed; hence this found its way to the cashier too, where it was carefully wrapped in bubble wrap and placed in a bag. Of which more later.

2.00pm: After a desultory wander round a few more shops we both felt hot and rather dispirited. The discordant noise out in the street and the sheer number of people was getting to us.

"Let's go home," said Shaun, and I readily agreed.

2.45pm: It was good to come into our quiet, peaceful house. Having moved home last October, this was the first anniversary at Knaphill rather than Addlestone, where James was born and brought up, and we both agreed it felt different in some indefinable way. There is much of a 'fresh start' about moving. You bring in your shared experiences and memories to a new home, but at the same time you are laying down new foundations of memory too. This is the first time Shaun and I have bought a house just for the two of us and we like the self-indulgence of that, at the same time missing the hurly burly of having youngsters around.

It is good that we have frequent visits from the younger generation to keep us young at heart!

As we got out of the car, unfortunately Shaun dropped the bag containing the glass candlestick and there was an ominous clinking sound. When we looked, the base of the piece was shattered into myriad pieces. Poor Shaun, he looked stricken. I felt close to tears. Suddenly this item assumed massive importance in the day. But I said, "Never mind, we can replace it another time," whilst all the while my mind was shouting that it had to be today.
Shaun must have read this because out of the goodness of his dear heart, he said he would go straight off to our nearest Marks and Spencer store to replace the item.
Though I protested feebly that it 'really didn't matter' (when it evidently did!) he would brook no argument.

3.00pm: Once Shaun left, I actually felt it was good for both of us to have a bit of breathing space on such an emotionally loaded day. I spent a while looking at all the wonderful tributes to James' memory on Facebook and reading the kind and heartfelt messages from so many people. It is incredible that eight years on, my son engenders responses to me, from so many people he never met. There were messages from France, South Africa, three different states of Australia – Perth, Melbourne and Sydney, the USA and of course here at home. Quite overwhelming.

I took myself away from the computer and applied myself to mundane tasks like preparing the vegetables for dinner (although it was a hot day we had agreed to have a roast chicken dinner – more comfort food) and then I cleaned the shower room.

Now that is a funny thing and once again is an echo of Shaun's grief processing – whenever I carry out that most commonplace of chores I feel my mind is absolutely free to wander and today I thought about James all the time I was doing it.

This did not make me feel sad, rather there was a comfort in it. I found myself having a brief conversation with him as though he had been with us in person at the riverside, rather than just in spirit.

"Well son, what did you think of it in Kingston today? How did it feel?"

Of course I had to imagine his response, but what I heard in my mind was, "I would say, mum, it was good to see so many people there enjoying themselves.

I like that I am remembered. I like that strangers read my plaque. I like that so many people send you messages and you benefit from their love and support. In particular, I like that you and Shaun have made sure that the area is safer now for everybody. I would hate to think of anyone else needlessly losing life there, particularly a little one."

James loved children. He would have made a fine primary school teacher and I always think of his connection to children, particularly when I see toddlers in buggies. He had such a knack of hunkering down on their level to talk to them. If a child was complaining in the supermarket, James would spend ages pulling silly faces to make the child laugh; it was just the kind of person he was. I miss his silly, touching humour and compassion, more than I can say.

4.00pm: Shaun arrived home with an intact candle holder and a bouquet of flowers for me. 'Guilt flowers,' he said. There was really no need but I was pleased just the same. Whilst Shaun prepared dinner, I spent time flitting about on the computer and seeing the messages still arriving; it seemed every five minutes there would be a new note to read.

I saw that Stella had posted a photo of herself and James and she was receiving many messages from her friends too. She wrote: "8 years ago today...unbelievable. Time might be a sort of healer but I still think about and miss my little brother as much as ever."

I was particularly touched by the note from one of her old school friends, which said, "8 years on and there is still so many people thinking of him today; that says a lot about James and what a special person he was. Thinking of you xxx."

My sister-in-law posted a lovely photo of a candle with a humming bird, writing, "For James. 8 years since you passed away; the flame representing the warmth we always feel thinking of you and humming bird for the joy you always spread. Always missing you xxx."

6.00pm: Now I decided it was time to light the candle for James. In fact I lit two candles, the one we bought today especially for him, and another one – placed in the new glass candle holder – for all the other youngsters lost to us too soon. I spent some time sitting quietly just thinking about them all.

7.00pm: It may be surprising but Shaun and I both made great inroads into our chicken dinners and felt content afterwards, if very tired. We agreed that the day had been difficult but manageable and settled to read the newspapers in our usual Sunday evening manner, with the television on quietly in the background. Suddenly, Shaun said to me, "You know, for whatever reason, I found today's anniversary one of the hardest to bear. I don't know why."

He had obviously been mulling over the day whilst ostensibly relaxing in front of the TV and I felt for him as he had appeared so calm and unruffled. It is easy to judge that someone is not feeling things as deeply as you are, when they do not show it outwardly. I leaned into him and we sat in quiet contemplation, each supporting the other.

9.00pm: Now I began to feel emotionally exhausted by the sheer efforts of the day. I had uploaded one of my photos from Kingston which gave rise to another flurry of comments and I took one last look at all the Facebook messages before closing down the computer and my phone with a feeling of relief.

Another anniversary over. Incredibly, it is the eighth time we have done this, the eighth time of observing our own special rituals, visiting the places we need to visit in our hearts and physically.

It gets easier in some respects. The passage of time lends distance to the raw emotions of new grief– thank goodness. When I go to Kingston I try just to see it as it is now, not the way it was in 2005 when our loss was new. The area was scruffy and unsafe, and it is due to what happened to James and our following actions that it is the place we see now.

But the visit to Kingston, the imagery imprinted on my mind from the riverside area and James' plaque, serve to underline our loss. The absence from our lives of that blithe, free spirit which is our darling James. I hold dear the joy, the laughter and the tears that 19 years of the privilege of knowing the love of my son gave to me. His life touched and brought joy to many and above all, he leaves us with memories of a life too short, but a life well-lived.

In Loving Memory
of
James Edward Clark
11 September 1985 - 28 July 2005

'We do not measure his life in years,
But by the endless love and joy he brought to us

Do Not Despair

For every tear you cry, mum
I will send you a smile
And memories of sunlit fun
Will comfort you a while
I need to let you know I'm there
Because you only half believeBut many things with you I
share
To prove I'll never leave
Rainbows, that after showers shine
White feathers, fluttering to the ground
Heed these as my loving signs
Which tell you that I'm still around
The dancing flight of butterflies
Or echoes of my voice you hear
Should not disturb you or surprise
They are proof that I am near
For every sleepless night you spend
I'll give you dreams to cherish
To show you that there is no end
I've moved on; but do not perish
And in the quiet of evening's calm
When milling thoughts subside
I'll surround you with my light, like balm
Forever now, I am by your side.

Andrea Corrie, 2008

Chapter 10

Railings, What Railings?

"I learned that if one has the vision of a clear objective in prospect, it is possible simultaneously to concentrate on the diversities of achievement and the time-consuming matter of grieving. Giving up on either was not an option."

Andrea Corrie

The day after James was found in the river, we were taken by our police liaison officers to Kingston so that we could see for ourselves where the tragedy happened. We were utterly shocked when we saw the riverside area and the lack of any safety measures there. The towpath was paved and there was a sheer drop to the river along a stretch directly opposite the nightclub, where James had spent his last evening with his friends. The exit steps from the nightclub lead directly to the river edge, although we were later told that the club staff tried to direct members of the public away from this exit at closing time; there is another exit that leads towards the town.

Between Kingston Bridge and the pub that marks the end of this particular leisure area, there are two sets of shallow steps leading down to the water, presumably for ease of access to and from boats. There was a single lifebelt along the path and the lighting appeared poor. CCTV cameras appeared to be trained on the nightclub, restaurant and pub that are along this stretch of the river.

Facing towards the bridge, the footpath was narrowed due to the presence of mature trees, and the height of the trees would obscure the view of the CCTV cameras were they trained onto the waterside.

In the midst of my anguish and pain I vowed, "This is going to change and I am going to make it happen so no-one else goes through this."

Our police liaison officers warned us that there was 'incident tape' across the area of the steps, which is where James was brought from the water and where the forensic team would do their part of the investigation. I had a bizarre moment of feeling as though we were actors taking part in a crime film because my mind literally could not process the reality of what we were seeing and experiencing.

I think that our first visit to the riverside remains one of the worst moments of loss.

At this stage, we had scanty information as to precisely what happened to James. I had so many questions: Was he pushed or did he fall? Why was he at the water's edge? He was a strong swimmer. How was it that he couldn't save himself?

To an extent, these questions have been answered for me over a period of time. Despite a thorough police investigation, there was no evidence to suggest that anyone meant James any harm that night. His mobile phone signal ceased shortly after his two groups of friends divided to take taxis, which suggests he was already in the water.

Each group of his friends thought he was with the other, which is why no alarm was raised at the time.

I frequently affirm that I do not blame any of James' friends for not noticing he was missing from the group, given that there was undoubtedly a throng of youngsters exiting from the nightclub at closing time.

My own supposition is that James simply went in the wrong direction – it was dark and he had been drinking all evening. He did not know Kingston well. I believe he lost his footing and fell into the river.

I do not believe, and there has never been any indication, that anyone witnessed his fall. There is a degree of comfort in knowing that his death was a pure accident and that no-one wished him harm. I have read of parents who can find it in themselves to forgive those who harmed their children, but I do not consider it is in me to be that generous of spirit.

As time went on, I learned a little about the mechanism of drowning and there is some comfort in knowing from what I have gleaned that it is often a very quick passing. The shock of cold water combined with alcohol intake would have led rapidly to unconsciousness and as soon as a breath is taken under the surface, which is a reflex reaction to the shock of immersion, the lungs fill with water, and there is little hope of being able to recover oneself.

These facts, difficult though they are to consider, were borne out by the post mortem which was performed to establish what happened to James and the conclusion was, not unexpectedly, that he had lost his life through accidental drowning.

Soon after our visit to the riverside, I contacted Kingston Council. As I have mentioned, many years ago I worked for this particular authority and it was helpful that a former colleague still works there; she was able to put me into contact with the right people.

For the benefit of those who are unfamiliar with the workings of local authorities, council officers are those employees of the council who work in various community departments and directorates, such as housing, environment, planning etc.

They prepare and present information to the elected councillors, who work together with the council's chief executive and officers via committees and meetings of the council to arrive at the decisions that ultimately control the capital expenditure allocated through set budgets from central government. Thus, our local councils work on behalf of the electorate in all community matters.

From the outset, we felt that we were effectively pushing on an open door with the council. However, I received some pessimistic news from the coroner when he told me that I was unlikely to succeed in getting the authority to agree to putting in railings along that stretch of the riverside because "it has been suggested before and it was not aesthetically acceptable." This was like a red rag to a bull as far as I was concerned and made me even more determined to effect change.

Prior to James' inquest which was held in October 2005, I was disappointed to receive a negative response from our local Member of Parliament, to whom it was suggested I write for support. As James' accident did not occur within his constituency boundary, our MP passed my letter on to the local MP for Kingston upon Thames, who promptly passed it back again as she said that, "Parliamentary convention dictates that Members of Parliament may only take up cases brought by their own constituents."

I found this response very upsetting, but in fact we managed to deal with it at local authority level.

The only way I could plan a strategy was as far as possible to detach myself emotionally from the reasons I was doing this, but it was extremely difficult to do at the time. I knew that effecting change through the local authority would take a while but it was a challenge that I was prepared to meet head on. I felt driven to do it and nothing was going to make me deviate from the quest.

Through our lobbying and frequent liaison, the council, the police and the licensed trade all worked together in a supportive and cohesive fashion on our behalf.

During the time I was considering how best to approach the relevant authorities and assessing my feelings about the outcome of the campaign, which was likely to take years, I was sent the following story, which seemed particularly apposite and spurred me on to action.

The Starfish Story

Once upon a time, there was a wise man who used to go to the ocean to do his writing. He had a habit of walking on the beach before he began his work.

One day, as he was walking along the shore, he looked down the beach and saw a human figure moving like a dancer. He smiled to himself at the thought of someone who would dance to the day, and so he walked faster to catch up.

As he got closer, he noticed that the figure was that of a young man, and that what he was doing was not dancing at all. The young man was reaching down to the shore, picking up small objects, and throwing them into the ocean. He came closer still and called out, "Good morning! May I ask what it is that you are doing?"

The young man paused, looked up, and replied "Throwing starfish into the ocean."

"I must ask, then, why are you throwing starfish into the ocean?" asked the somewhat startled wise man.

To this, the young man replied, "The sun is up and the tide is going out. If I don't throw them in, they'll die."

Upon hearing this, the wise man commented, "But, young man, do you not realise that there are miles and miles of beach and there are starfish all along every mile? You can't possibly make a difference!"

At this, the young man bent down, picked up yet another starfish, and threw it into the ocean. As it met the water, he said, "It made a difference for that one."

I contacted the council very soon after James' death, and by December 2005, the preliminary report into river safety, commissioned by the chief executive of the council following committee liaison and recommendations from HM Coroner, was produced.

It transpired that the area had not been subject to particular scrutiny since a RoSPA (Royal Society for the Prevention of Accidents) report was commissioned in 1993, following a prior drowning.

At that time, recommendations were made for the installation of riverside railings in the area, together with fencing and safety improvements.

However, these measures were rejected as they "would have an unacceptable impact on the visual character and amenity of the area." This bore out what I had been told by the Coroner's Office.

Nevertheless, at this time, RoSPA's report identified a series of hazards in the area, including the presence of pubs and riverside restaurants and suggested that urgent action should be taken to introduce barriers to protect members of the public. The report concluded that the "situation should be regarded as high risk and action should be taken to place fixed waterside guardrailings of an anti-climb nature."

Further weight was applied to the situation in 1999 when RoSPA produced guidance entitled "*Safety at Inland Water Sites*" which suggests "the use of physical barriers where the risks associated with adjacent activities to the riverbank are increased by factors, including heavy access by the public and adjacent pubs and restaurants and a steep drop into water."

With the benefit of hindsight it is utterly galling to us that these recommendations, both in 1993 and later in 1999, were not acted upon by the council - but added a great deal of gravitas to our own pressure for action to take place. The risk assessment conclusion and recommended control measures contained in this initial report informed us that, "the situation should be regarded as high risk and action should be taken in line with the 1999 RoSPA guidelines and the 1993 RoSPA report to place fixed waterside guardrailings of an anti-climb nature, as originally proposed before the 1993 planning application (for restaurants in the area). Because of the heavy presence of the public and the likelihood of a direct fall into the river physical protection by guardrailings would be the only effective solution to reduce the risk."

In February 2006, we met with the council officers to discuss the report before it was presented for consideration by the Kingston Town Neighbourhood Committee. The proposal being put forward was for the next stage in the process: a feasibility study to be carried out to establish what safety measures were needed, how the works would be done, cost, timescale etc.

We were at that time gratified to learn that the council officers' view was that "there is every support for positive action so that some good will come from the tragic death of James."

I had an immense need to be part of the consultation and decision making process and we were invited to attend the meeting of the Kingston Town Neighbourhood Committee, comprising some twelve members of the council, three from each of the local wards (constituency divisions by area), on 8 February 2006.

When we met with the council officers we discussed the premise that I would like to add some weight to the decision making process by stating my case. This was viewed positively and during the meeting I was invited to speak.

I was extremely nervous but I knew that I had to have my voice heard.

I prepared a statement and read it to the committee, saying, "I appreciate the opportunity to address the meeting. The committee will know that we met on an informal basis with the council officers last week. We found the meeting very positive and we acknowledge the efforts that have so far been made.

If everything that has been promised comes to fruition, we will feel that our efforts have not been in vain.

Having read the safety report, it is difficult for us to turn our minds away from the belief that had the previously recommended action been taken, what befell my son would have been far less likely.

The most positive accomplishment that we can hope for is to ensure that measures are taken to prevent further loss of life, and it is in this regard that we urge you, as a committee, to approve and support such action to the fullest possible extent.

We hope that the momentum that has already been generated by the Authority in their deliberations can continue to grow and take the matter forward to a constructive conclusion.

I also hope the committee appreciates my need to feel that I am contributing to the progression of this issue, through participating in the different stages of the process.

On a more personal note, it is impossible for me to express the sense of loss that comes with being a bereaved parent; I hardly need say that it is against the natural order of life. For me, part of trying to come to terms with my loss is to do whatever is within my power to prevent another family living through such a tragedy."

I felt that my presentation was well received and all the recommendations within the report were accepted that evening. These were:

Agreement to commission a feasibility study in respect of a comprehensive upgrading of safety and other control measures at this popular part of the riverside walk and Agreement by the Director of Finance to make provision within the 2006/2007 Capital Programme to allow any safety features or improved lighting to be undertaken at the earliest opportunity following consideration and approval by the Neighbourhood Committee of the findings of the feasibility study.

Following this, the next stage was for the feasibility study to be completed.

Time passed and although it appeared to the outside world that not much was happening, I received regular progress reports from the council officers and was reassured that the study was indeed underway.

By September 2006, the feasibility study and a further report from RoSPA commissioned by the consultants undertaking the study, to update their recommendations, were complete.

The remit of the feasibility study report asked for the undertaking of a "comprehensive feasibility study as to the provision of pedestrian health and safety control measures to minimise the dangers posed by the river Thames and to improve public safety and awareness of the inherent dangers and risks to pedestrians associated with the location of this watercourse in close proximity of a busy pedestrian thoroughfare."

Specific implications for the council were made clear in a statement that "a lack of funds was no defence for a lack of safety precautions, particularly when they had been previously recommended." The report also made the point that the local authority actively encouraged visitors to the site and that, this being the case, the health and safety precautions must be "particularly effective."

The recommendations within the finalised reports were approved by the council in September 2006.

The council agreed to:

- Provision of barriers along the relevant part of the riverside walk
- Provision of handrails and barriers to two flights of steps
- Protection of steps above dwarf brick walls in two areas of the walkway
- Improvement in visibility and contrast of the steps (through using different building materials).
- Provision of benches to focus pedestrian flow towards and away from certain areas
- Increased lighting provision
- Repair of grab chains already in situ
- Directing exit customers away from the riverside and towards town as they leave the nightclub
- Increase in life saving equipment
- Management of local business/Pubwatch activity to increase safety awareness and training of staff

- Information to the public about the dangers of inland waterways

- Regular site monitoring

One of the hurdles we had to overcome was a feeling by some of the local councillors that if these measures were implemented at this site, there may be a case for them to be instituted at other sites. However, our concern was in the immediate area close to Kingston bridge rather than a wider area. We had the full support of the head of Neighbourhood Services, who presented his departmental report to the committee, including his own observational comments, stating, "The riverside is an important pedestrian route and gateway into the town centre and as such safety must be paramount. The dangers associated with the infrastructure of the riverside walk at this point have not changed since the issue of riverside safety was last considered in 1993.

However, since this date, the riverside walk has been completed and now offers a greater attraction of leisure venues. As a result, usage of this area has grown tremendously in terms of usage by those using licensed premises, the nightclub and those using the walkway to reach the town centre and residential accommodation.

It is also important to recognise that at this point the riverside walk consists of a vertical drop of two metres into the water, which in some places is two metres deep and fast flowing. This combination of usage and the physical elements is unique within Kingston's stretch of riverside and this alone warrants consideration of additional safety features not relevant to other parts of the riverside.

As clearly identified, the council has a statutory duty in relation to the health and safety of members of the public and others such as its own employees and contracted staff. The commissioning of the three reports (since the outset) provide a clear indication of the council's recognition of its duties. The findings arising from the commissions cannot be ignored and appropriate action must now be taken."

The head of Neighbourhood Services concluded by endorsing the recommendations arising from the feasibility study.

This was the crucial decision arising from all the work leading up to this point.

We were hugely relieved that the committee approved the report and agreed to the expenditure required to adopt the recommendations within it.

Local press coverage did not elicit negative response, which was pleasing, given the history we had been given of local residents objecting to barriers on purely aesthetic grounds.

Over time, the phases of the works were gradually completed. We had requested a commemorative plaque to be placed at the riverside in memory of James. We had full consultation with the council over this and after we attended the site to finalise our decision on its placement, they arranged for it to be put in place in September 2007, just prior to James' birthday.

The wording on the slate plaque reads:

"In loving memory of James Edward Clark.
11 September 1985 – 28 July 2005.
We do not measure his life in years
But by the endless love and joy he brought to us."

A symbolic butterfly is in the top right hand corner of the plaque.

We placed flowers at the plaque on James' birthday - his 22nd - and I reflected that this was the culmination of a successful campaign to provide a lasting legacy, which would mean that no other family should have to suffer the loss that we live with.

It would be impossible to measure the effects of the increased safety of the area, but there is no doubt that, like the man throwing the starfish into the ocean, we made a difference.

With the completion of the resurfacing works and installation of improved lighting in March 2008, the project was effectively complete from the point of view of building works and improvements to the safety level and aesthetics of the riverside. At this time, I felt that I could withdraw my energies from Kingston as my job on James' behalf was, to all intents and purposes, done.

I recall feeling a sense of relief combined with exhaustion after the culmination of the many emails, consideration of correspondence and meetings that had led to this point. Throughout our campaign, I kept all my email contacts updated regularly and it helped me to document progress. Not only that, but I knew that the unseen support from all the recipients of my regular bulletins helped me to process my grief, on a level of practicality rather than spirituality. By this I mean that through focusing my energies on a business-like campaign I was ticking off boxes with the works being undertaken and at the same time I feel that my mind was ticking off boxes taking me forward on my grief path.

Our frequent visits to Kingston town centre and the riverside throughout the campaign period helped to desensitise me from the appalling shock of James' death in the river. On each visit, as we approached Kingston itself, my stomach would flip somersaults and my heart was heavy, but I always came away with a sense of achievement and relief that another visit was over. In time, I could look in a less blinkered way at the whole picture of leisure at the riverside, and feel less resentful of the people who enjoyed the environment heedless of our personal tragedy. After all, there was no reason for them to know what we have been through to arrive at the place where we are today.

In January 2009, the head of Neighbourhood Services at Kingston Council sent me an email, saying: "You may recall that as part of the Riverside Project there was always a proposal to promote awareness of the dangers posed by the river through the production of either an appropriate leaflet or poster.

In discussion with key river based agencies, it has proved difficult to agree a style or type of awareness leaflet that would really target the key at risk group of young people and to make a link with the associated danger of alcohol-induced impairment of judgement of safety in and around the riverside.

We felt it was essential to target the safety awareness campaign to the 'at risk' groups as our experience is that a middle of the road general campaign tends to miss the problem area and therefore adds no benefits to what we are trying to achieve.

After due consideration and working in partnership with the Thames Landscape Strategy organisation we have agreed to produce a beer mat that can, and will be, used by all licensed premises along the riverside.

The beer mat will be double-sided containing important information on reporting an incident through the emergency services and will give the 999 (UK emergency) number and advice on whom to ask for and what information will assist the operator. The reverse of the beer mat will follow the highly successful road safety format showing a graphic image to hit home the message.

The scheme has received the full support of the local police who are keen on the beer mat style awareness campaign as targeting groups who are most at risk.

The council hope to produce quantities of the beer mats in the very near future and therefore I thought it was appropriate to advise you of this initiative now before the beer mats are put into use.

I hope you will be supportive of this initiative, its aims and of course the outcome objectives. I would be happy to discuss this with you if you wanted to clarify any of the proposals."

I was pleased to be offered the opportunity to contribute my thoughts on this campaign and shared the design and wording with Nancy Rigg of the Drowning Support Network. Together we formulated some minor amendments that were incorporated into the design and the promotion was launched later that year, feedback indicating that it was a valuable tool in the armoury of water safety. It has become evident in the years since our initial involvement that the council and other authorities have not slackened off their efforts to maintain safety within Kingston Town Centre.

I believe that James' death was a catalyst for change at the riverside and this in turn has evolved into a broadening of the safety measures that are now deemed applicable in any town centre where the demographic includes a high number of young people.

Kingston has a university and its population is diverse and cosmopolitan. It appears that the authorities take their duty of care very seriously these days, when the dangers to large groups of people socialising together are at a high level. I recently contacted the council again enquiring as to what has been achieved since we effectively bowed out of our personal involvement with river safety in Kingston. I received the following reply from the officer with whom we have dealt all along. Formerly the head of Neighbourhood Services, he now holds the title of 'Capability Lead – Community/Strategic Business'. He said:

"In response to your request and for ease of reference I have listed all the activities I can think of that we have introduced since the railings were erected.

- Completion and regular update of a River Safety Plan (The Plan has been shared across London by London Fire Brigade as good practice)
- River Safety Audit in November 2011
- Open Water Access Assessment March 2012
- A River Safety Group, which I Chair, meets four times a year and is comprised of council, police, fire brigade, RNLI (Royal National Lifeboat Institution), Town Centre Neighbourhood and university representatives
- River safety training for employees of premises located next to river (now held twice a year May and September). Trained door staff have already used their training to save lives when young people chose to go into the water and got into trouble
- Liaison with licenced premises on riverside to provide them with lifesaving equipment – throw ropes etc (annual audit and replacement of equipment by town centre management committee)
- Improved riverside safety signage with emergency information clearly displayed
- RNLI attending Kingston university on a regular basis to talk with students about the dangers of open water space
- We continue to distribute the beer mats and posters on an annual basis – as you know a very powerful message
- The council's CCTV control room now has direct radio contact with RNLI so if an incident is reported we can go directly to RNLI as well as through the 999 system

Whilst not directly river related we have also introduced a number of initiatives to help people who have had a good night's entertainment to remain safe:

- Taxi Rank marshalls/kiosks at key points to ensure people get into a licensed cab/taxi only and get home safely

- Street pastors who wander the town until the early hours supporting people who either have run out of money, lost their phones, need water or have minor injuries from falls – they also provide flipflops for the many young women who break or lose their heels every week and are found walking barefoot around the town

The town also gained the first ever Purple Flag accreditation, which has since been renewed annually three times. Purple Flag is a scheme that recognises good practice, safety measures, a safe town centre after dark and good customer care.

As a general comment I would say that the whole issue of river safety and preventative measures has been high profile and remains a key area upon which the emergency services, the council and Kingston town centre management wish to focus resources to avoid future incidents of any type and try to educate young people on the dangers of the river, particularly when they have had a drink."

I feel that we were very fortunate on a personal level in our dealings with Kingston Council as we were met with compassion from the outset. All our requests were carefully considered and although the cynic in me says that the council was forced to act by legislation, there was never any sense that they would not give the situation the attention it deserved.

It is a measure of their ethos that we were kept informed at all stages and I believe that the officers concerned felt a personal sense of responsibility to ensure that we were not disappointed with the eventual outcomes.

I know from my dealings with the council that James' plaque is regularly inspected on an informal basis and I am happy to know that someone is keeping a 'weather eye' on it.

It was interesting for us to see, when we visited the riverside this summer, that the area where James died is being redeveloped. There are to be a number of new restaurants and places to socialise. It is gratifying for us to know that when this new redevelopment is in place, the level of safety for the customers will be much higher than previously...although this also holds a great deal of poignancy.

I no longer feel the need to visit Kingston regularly. I love it, though, when we hear that others have been to the riverside and paid a visit to the area.

We go to the riverside each July and place flowers at James' plaque on his anniversary. The area is now lighter, brighter and above all safer. As far as aesthetics are concerned, the entire riverside project has enabled many more people to enjoy all the facilities on offer in a safe and convivial manner.

Sadly, James was not the first young man to lose his life in the Thames at Kingston. But I am hopeful that the end result of our campaign will fulfil our original objective, which was to do our utmost to prevent further loss of life in this area.

I am not alone in campaigning for change as a result of loss.

After her son Tom's funeral, my TCF friend, Linda, told me that she felt as though she had fallen off the side of the planet, into a dark pit of despair where there was no colour. There she remained for almost a year.

Then, gradually, some chinks of light appeared and very gradually colour started to creep back in.

Eight weeks after Tom's death Linda became aware of a young woman, Sarah Bond, who also died in a quad bike accident in New Zealand. The two mothers became friends and later allies in challenging the New Zealand authorities. They were able to support one another in the way only bereaved parents can – each with true understanding of the other's situation.

With the arrival of the accident report on Tom's death from the Department of Labour in New Zealand, Linda realised she had to act.

"The report was full of holes," Linda told me. "It was inaccurate and amateurish. I took it to our local MP at the time, Mr Humfrey Malins, and he wrote to the New Zealand authorities on our behalf. Unfortunately, there was a distinct lack of response at that time.

I began to monitor the New Zealand press online and realised that there were a very high number of quad bike accidents and deaths. I knew I had to act to try and prevent further loss of life, but it was an enormous and daunting task."

Tom and Sarah's deaths were treated quite differently by the New Zealand authorities. Tom died in the workplace, and Sarah had been on a leisure trip so her accident was attributed to the 'risks of extreme tourism'.

However, the end result is much the same, as Linda puts it, "There is quite simply a general failing in all areas of Health and Safety in New Zealand. You would think that a commonwealth country would be similar to the UK, but they fall short of our standards in so many ways.

We have made progress, but it has been hard won. I can now say that everyone in New Zealand knows Tom's name. There has been a major review of Health and Safety in New Zealand after a Government commissioned independent review publicly labelled their system a 'national disgrace'. Yes, my voice has been heard, but I have to keep on keeping on...making sure there is an attitude shift."

Tom's inquest in the UK did not take place until January 2013. Linda prepared for it as you would prepare for a military operation. She said that the local Coroner really listened to her and wrote to the Coroner in New Zealand with ten recommendations for positive change. This was doubly important because the inquest in Essex into Sarah Bond's death had decided that her death was due to an isolated accident. Given all the evidence gathered in New Zealand, this was clearly not the case and so it was as important for the Bond family as it was for Linda's family to get a positive result.

Linda and I agree that the world keeps turning even though it has temporarily stopped for us with the death of our sons. But we find the strength from somewhere to challenge the injustices and wrongs that surround the loss of our boys.

My own campaign at Kingston riverside was small and local compared to Linda's international battle and I have great admiration for all she has achieved, and will continue to achieve going forward, on behalf of many families worldwide.

The riverside at Kingston before our campaign

The riverside at Kingston as it is today

Chapter 11

Triumph Over Adversity

*"Grief never disappears completely. You slog your way
through it somehow, to emerge marked, scarred and
wearied. Then sorrow settles in your heart like a nascent
seed, poised to flourish the moment it is fed with a memory.
Faith and hope set the bloom in beauty."*

Andrea Corrie

Very soon after James died, I felt an overwhelming need to
have contact with other parents who were experiencing life
after the loss of a teenager. I felt so alone and believed that
if I could be in touch with others who were further along
the line than I was, this would bring a measure of comfort.
Through a mention in one of our condolence cards, I
discovered the Compassionate Friends, an organisation,
which is run *by* bereaved parents *for* bereaved parents and I
joined the online forum.

Reading the posts of other bereaved parents was both heart
breaking and uplifting and I began to realise that every
child loss affects each individual in an entirely different
way. This is despite there being a great deal of common
ground; the incredible pain and the yearning to be able to
touch or talk to one's child 'just one more time'.

On joining TCF, members are assigned a contact who is
several years post loss, and my contact wrote positively to
me about the pain of loss, saying that in time the intensity
would start to diminish, but very, very slowly. I clutched
eagerly at any intimation that this dreadful abyss of early
loss would not be forever.

I looked for other mothers of 19-year-olds on the TCF online forum, and I was drawn to the positive and uplifting posts by Sandy, an American lady living in Brixham with her husband Keith. She had lost her son David. I contacted her directly by email and we soon discovered we had plenty in common besides the obvious starting point of our loss. Sandy too had a daughter, David's sister Kelly, and two stepchildren.

Both our husbands (and in fact Sandy herself) worked for British Telecom. We soon began emailing each other regularly and our exchanges held the intimacy of people who have never met but who understand each other's point of view.

David also died in an accident, caused when his friend who was driving his car and was over the alcohol limit, ran into a bridge abutment. It is a credit to Sandy's warmth and compassion that she said, "The driver was charged with vehicular manslaughter (in the USA) and had a year in jail. I do not feel anger at him or blame him, surprisingly perhaps, but they were all out that night and just didn't use their heads, which isn't uncommon at that age.

It's just such a tragic waste of young life...for both of our boys...and we are left to survive through it. I am also trying to focus on my lovely boy and the 19 years I had with him. I'd rather have had him as long as I did and then go through this agony than not have him at all. Still, how to make it through this; I'm still struggling with it at every moment."

Sandy went on to say something that echoed with my own feelings early on, "I feel so isolated sometimes with other people because they don't understand, they certainly don't want to hear about it and their eyes glaze over when I mention his name (thank God my family doesn't do this but others do). I love to talk about David, love to say his name and it's difficult when others would rather not talk about him. Have you found that to be the case?"

Sandy and I found we could relate to each other with our experiences which followed very similar paths and we both vented our feelings in emails which I am sure helped us immeasurably.

I loved Sandy's resolute character. In an email exchange once when I was writing about someone who was making my life difficult, she said, "Andrea, you don't need toxic people in your life. Break off contact and take away that pressure."

This turned out to be very sagacious advice and I have passed on her words to many people over the years, to good effect.

Some months after we first connected in late 2005, I realised Sandy was seriously ill when she made references to various hospital visits. Eventually she told me that she had a recurrence of the breast cancer, which had formerly been treated prior to David's death. She said she had hesitated to tell me "in case it detracted from our discussions about our boys" confirming that her generosity of spirit was even greater than I had previously thought. She was a very selfless and considerate woman and her main concerns were always for her family and those around her as she went through treatment for her illness.

She was always amazingly upbeat, as she wrote to me during her treatment, "The radiotherapy starts out making things hurt worse, but then they start improving rapidly which is where I am now; the pain has reduced significantly so I'm very pleased and I'm feeling quite strong too."

Typically she went on to ask me how I was feeling and how I was coping with the upcoming anniversary of James' death, before saying, "Oh, I forgot to mention that I'm running the 5K Race for Life in Torquay next Saturday. My youngest stepdaughter is running it with me. Since I really do feel on the mend, I'm determined to run the whole 5K and not walk at all so please keep your fingers crossed for me."

Sandy was very focused on always trying to help others and I know that she was instrumental in setting up local support groups for women with breast cancer.

We met in person only twice. The first time we both attended a grief workshop in Totnes, Devon, with another mutual friend from TCF. At this workshop, incredibly out of a group of six, there were four women who had lost 19-year-old boys, which made for an emotionally loaded but ultimately helpful day.

Sadly, it became evident that Sandy was not going to be cured of her cancer, but she remained positive, bright and as compassionate as ever. She and her husband stayed with us for a weekend in the summer of 2006, which was an occasion for much conversation and laughter.

Unfortunately, she had to go into hospital several times during November and December, and in January 2007 she passed away. I was honoured to be asked to speak at her funeral and also touched to meet her lovely daughter Kelly, who lives near Atlanta, Georgia and despite her struggles through losing both her brother and her mum resolutely forges through her life and recently married.

I was asked to say a few words about our friendship and also given this poem by Henry Van Dyke to read at Sandy's funeral:

"I am standing upon the seashore. A ship at my sides spreads her white sails in the morning breeze and starts for the blue ocean.
She is an object of beauty and strength and I stand and watch her until, at length, she is only a ribbon of white cloud just where the sea and sky come to mingle with each other.
Then someone at my side says,
'There! She's gone!'
Gone where? Gone from my sight - that is all.
She is just as large in mast and hull and spar as she was when she left my side, and just as able to bear her load of living freight to the place of destination.
Her diminished size is in me, not in her, and just at the moment when someone at my side says,
'There! She's gone!'
There are other voices ready to take up the glad shout
'There! She comes!'"

This sums up Sandy very well, for she had a strong belief in the afterlife and I am quite sure she was comforted to think that she would be reunited with David after her passing. Her concern was not for herself or her suffering, but for the family and friends she left behind.

She was one of those rare people whom make an indelible impression through their positive attributes, warmth and compassion. She was a truly inspirational and strong lady and I feel privileged to have known her.

Kelly has inherited her mother's ability to express herself in writing and she says of her losses: "Grieving the loss of my younger brother, David, and my mom stirred up a laundry list of emotions, none that I think we could really prepare for until we approach what initially felt like tall mountains to be climbed, and by the way, I'm pretty scared of heights. It was a mountain that included trails where I was going through the various stages of grief. Some trails were totally uphill and rockier than I ever expected, and at others I would come to a resting point, at times even with a new pond to drink from or another mountain climber that could empathise with me or perhaps give me words of wisdom. But the trail I most vividly remember was that of my new identity. I shared a close relationship with both David and mom. My big sister instinct was always to protect my brother; what was I to do with that energy and those emotions after his death? When mom passed on, I struggled with the hole that was left in my heart that only her presence could fill. When life was at its all time highs and then its painful lows, I still wanted my mom. It was almost as if I was meeting a new me...composed of different identities, yet still the same girl.

Although I never wanted to be a daring mountain climber, I certainly didn't want to climb this mountain of grief solo. That led to undoubtedly the most important aspect of my grief process; my faith in God and its realness. No longer was the idea of heaven just a far distant dreamland that I learned about in a pew. It was real and the concept of life's fragility was now so clear.

Also, as I look back, I can confidently say, although the process of grief was not a cookie cutter process, I felt God's presence. I know He never left me. There was something so peaceful about knowing life was bigger than this, bigger than this Earthly life we wake up to each morning.

I do think that this climb has had its share of good and bad. I'm still on it; in fact I think I'll be on it until I pass on. Missing David and mom will continue to be present in the various stages of life I will enter. There have been and will continue to be new trails I will venture onto that will remind me of how much I miss them and wish they were here. But I will forge on, knowing that I'm not alone, knowing that if I enter a painful trail, a new one will soon be ahead, maybe even with a bench to rest a while.

As the years go by, I have grown more and more accustomed to this journey. The grief journey is not something I feel you can prepare for, but to me, it is a journey that gets easier with time. I still miss mom and David and wish they could be here, but I'm joyful for the times we had together. I also find myself in a place where I'm joyful for my future ahead, knowing that my mountain climb, as well as my mom and brother have impacted a part of who I am."

In an ideal world, when a child dies, we should have a supportive network around us of partner, family and friends. I am lucky to have been able to draw on such a network, but some of my post loss friends have not.

One friend, Lin, told me she found it helped her to express her feelings in poetry as she could not vent to anyone close to her.

The following two poems were written during the early years of her loss and describe eloquently the mixed emotions that surround us when we are bereaved of our children.

I Look For You

I look for you, and there you are
In the furthest reaches of mind
Almost hidden, almost in view.
I can feel your presence
Yet I cannot see you.
My mind reaches out, touches you
In the way my hands cannot.
I long to hold your face in my hands
To whisper "I cannot breathe without you."
My mind screams
Craving your presence.
My heart calls softly
With a gentle tone.
I wait without patience
Listening for the sound of your Soul meeting mine
Still, we remain entwined in dance,
Apart, yet not.

A Grief Continued

Reality and memory mixed, once sharp lines on a white
board,
the divide no longer visible
Blue-flamed days of disassociated nothingness,
empty hours demanding a guilt against time.
Days move forward, the mind frozen, a helter-skelter
leading nowhere
Sharp spokes from a bicycle wheel dig into the mental skin
of remembrance
Too sharp to ignore, too painful to remove.
Throughout it all, white feathers fall from nowhere, a
shower of calm.

Grieving as a father also gives a different perspective. Shaun Hewitt is a Trustee of TCF and he describes his grief path following the loss of his son Oliver, honestly and from the heart:

"Now, my reason for going on. You know in a TV drama, when someone gets devastating news, and they fall to their knees bellowing; well I always thought that was done for dramatic effect. I now know that this can happen in reality.

I remember the phone call; I remember the hour-long drive to my son's home, and running up the road all the while believing it was a mistake. I remember not being able to park near the house due to the police cars, paramedics and an ambulance. I even remember walking into the house past a police officer at the bottom of the stairs still believing it wasn't happening. Until the second I saw my ex wife's face. And that's when I fell to my knees, bellowing.

There the similarity to TV drama ends. Two episodes later, I am *not* better, I am *not* over it, and I resent them for not having prepared me for what this hell is really like. Unfortunately, life's instruction book is missing that chapter too.

Through life, we will more than likely meet someone who has lost a parent, an aunt, even a husband or wife and somehow, this is 'normal' and we learn from it. But the chances are, even if we *have* met someone who has lost a child, we haven't dared look too closely, or to put ourselves in their place. Hence, when it happens to us, what? What now? What do I do? What? - someone tell me.

In the days following, I went into practical mode.
I arranged a funeral, (picking from wood samples on that afternoon, when I had varnished a similar piece of wood at work that morning before).

I closed bank accounts, I answered letters, I filled my time. Later I made a website for Oliver, I opened my garden for charity, I filled my time.

But sooner or later you have to stop, you have to give in to the grief, there is no way round it, you can't cheat it. That's when you need support.

I will ever bless the mother of Rosie Ross, (a beautiful young girl murdered in the centre of Birmingham, UK), who gave me the address of the charity website, TCF, a charity in which every member has lost a child or a sibling. My first tentative steps towards believing that I could have a future (however bleak it appeared) were when I talked to, and met other bereaved parents: people who *really* understood what I was going through.

It wasn't always spoken, but I knew they knew, and they knew that I knew. Being a gay dad wasn't an issue either. It didn't matter; I was a grieving dad.

Without the support of other bereaved parents, I have no idea where I'd be now. However kind and supportive my non-bereaved friends and family are, and continue to be, there is always that extra voice in my head saying, 'You don't really know what it's like, and I thank God you don't.'

With the greater acceptance of gay relationships, and people realising we are like everyone else at heart, my civil partner Paul is also more frequently seen for what he is -

Oliver's step dad. Within TCF as well as in a broader arena it is recognised that he is missing Oliver just as much as any parent, and it's not only me who has been robbed of the blessing of grandchildren; we both have.

When you lose an only child, you have to find another purpose for your life, another reason to continue taking up space. I've found my reason in doing my best to help other parents on this rocky road. It's not the life I envisioned, but it is a bearable life. I cannot contribute to the next generation, so I will help my contemporaries with the experience I have gained in the last seven years.

Oliver Thomas Hewitt was my only child, and he left on his 'awfully big adventure' in March 2006 aged 23. He died suddenly in his sleep from a heart virus. Always my reason for living, now my reason for going on."

Another bereaved parent who eloquently expresses her feelings is writer Jan Andersen. She analyses the unpredictable passage of grief, saying, "There is always the assumption that the pain of losing a child, grandchild or sibling will lessen with time, that the second year will be easier than the first, the third easier than the second and so on. It doesn't always happen in such a predictable fashion. When one loses a child, emotional triggers can bring an intense grief to the surface that is as raw and powerful as it was in the beginning, even years after the tragedy.

All child loss is devastating, but when the death was sudden and unexpected, shock and disbelief accompanies the grief. In the beginning, parents (and other family members) wonder how they will ever make it through another day and cannot even begin to entertain thoughts of years ahead without the child who has passed on.

The effect of shock is an inability to absorb or accept what has happened. When this shock wears off - at no pre-determined time - it is replaced by the brutal reality of what has happened.

Although I lost my son Kristian to suicide in 2002, I still remember with vivid clarity those first few days and months of indescribable agony. I had to find something that would make me put my feet on the floor every day; a new purpose in life. That purpose seemed obvious. I could not allow my son's suicide to cause me to give up on everyone; those I knew and those I didn't know who needed help, comfort and hope. My son bequeathed to me the love, compassion and forgiveness that he showed to so many when he was alive. This was a gift that I had to use to the best of my ability; a gift that could not be wasted. It would be an insult to my son's memory to give up on life and fail all the others who were dear to my heart. My suffering would be channelled constructively and would help create something positive from such a dreadful tragedy.

The one comforting thought that I try to dwell on is the knowledge that my son is at peace. All I ever wanted for my children was for them to be happy. I desperately wish that my son had not chosen death as a vehicle to happiness, but I know that he is no longer tortured. My belief that death of the body is not death of soul has been tremendously comforting, along with the constant signs I receive that he is still with me in spirit.

The day that Kristian passed over, I began writing the poem that was read out at his funeral three weeks later. How did I manage to form those words and channel such intense grief into something even vaguely comprehensible? What fuelled this creativity was an overpowering compulsion to honour my son and let the world know what a special young man he was, despite his faults, of which we all have many. What was the point in being a writer if I could not use my talents to pay tribute to Kristian in a personal way that no other ready-written verse could do? This was the very least that I could do for him.

A few weeks later, in addition to starting a book - *Chasing Death: Losing a Child to Suicide* - which was published in October 2009, I began creating a website to support both families who have lost a child, grandchild, sibling, friend or relative to suicide and people who may be feeling suicidal. Just being able to offer comfort to one family, or to prevent one person from ending their life would mean that Kristian had achieved something amazing.

Establishing the child suicide website was one of the most positive and constructive things I could have done. From small beginnings, the site grew into an incredible support network around the world, linking people with others in a similar situation and with organisations equipped to help both the suicidal and those who have experienced suicide within their family. In addition, as time has moved forward, I can speak to newly bereaved families from the perspective of someone who is several years further on in the grieving process.

These are my coping strategies, but grieving is an intensely personal journey, so each bereaved person has to find their own way of moving forward in the knowledge that they will eventually reach a point where thoughts of their child or loved one do not occupy every waking minute; a time when they accept that joy and sadness can co-exist."

One of the first people whom I met (virtually) on the TCF forum was Frances Speakman. Frances and her husband Mike devoted a great deal of time and energy to creating a lasting memorial. I asked Frances to describe their campaign.

"The idea for a Public Memorial Angel came about after we lost our beautiful eldest daughter Angela from a fatal asthma attack in February 2003. After the Requiem Mass held at St Augustine's Catholic Church in Barkingside, Ilford, we then had to face the very difficult service at the City of London Cemetery for the cremation of our beloved daughter. We found the staff there so kind and helpful, which in such difficult circumstances was so very much appreciated.

I had, over the years, visited this large Victorian cemetery, which is in Aldersbrook Road, Manor Park London E12 5DQ, many times in connection with research on soldiers who gave their lives during WWI, and noticed many of the beautiful, sculptured Victorian angel statues 'laid' on the grass for safety's sake, having come from unstable monuments.

I contacted Dr. Ian Hussein, the Director of the City of London Cemetery & Crematorium and put the idea to him of using one of these beautiful angel statues as a Public Memorial in memory of all our lost children, all ages, all religions. He welcomed this as a wonderful idea and said he would give it his full support and assistance. He told me they were piloting the reclamation and re-use of old abandoned monuments (in liaison with English Heritage and English Nature) under the guidance of their Heritage Advisory Panel.

I had already submitted a proposed inscription, which had been accepted, for a plaque to be mounted on the memorial. Also, ideas had been discussed as to a suitable location within the cemetery. It was proposed to have a specially designated area next to the memorial for parents to leave flowers etc. In March 2005, several angels that might be suitable were identified, though all needed restoration work. The next step was to wait to determine whether any were claimed by living relatives of the original owners. By November 2005, The Heritage Committee had given approval for one of these Victorian angels to be used.

To establish this memorial in memory of all our children, we needed to get wider general public support and importantly, financial contributions towards the costs. This was needed for the restoration of the chosen angel, the provision of a suitable base and the inscription plaque. Public subscription seemed most appropriate to confirm support for the memorial. The City of London Corporation agreed to pay for the upkeep and provide the land it will occupy. It is indeed a very safe and secure place to have this beautiful memorial, for bereaved parents to visit and to meet other parents for a cup of tea in the lovely café, which is just inside the main gate, and to chat about our beautiful, lost children as only bereaved parents can.

I asked the general public and bereaved parents groups, including the Compassionate Friends, to contact me by email or letter to register support for the memorial and if possible to donate towards its establishment. Also, our local newspaper, *The Ilford Recorder*, ran a couple of features about the project to reach a wider audience, and another just before the unveiling in 2009.

I set up a website with all the details on about the angel memorial and received in return tremendous support, donations and wonderful messages and cards. Dr. Hussein kindly donated to me 20 copies of a book, which had been recently published about the History of the City of London cemetery, how it came about and why it was needed.

He said all the money I made selling the books could go to the fund. I set up a bank account into which all donations towards the costs could be paid. Mike and I held fundraising lunches at our house, and made many visits to local shops asking for their support via items for the various raffle prizes - they were all very generous. The first lunch we held was attended mostly by good friends met through TCF. The lunch was lovely, with everyone enjoying the delicious food; I made a very special 'Compassionate Friends' cake with a golden candle; after this was lit we held a two minutes silence during which we all remembered our precious children. It was a lovely day, with good friends, and raised together with the raffle, a wonderful sum of over £400 towards this memorial. We held a St. George's day coffee morning, including lots of delicious cakes and were so lucky the weather held, and were able to sit in the garden. We raised another £110 towards the memorial.

After I had banked the money and other donations kindly given, Mike and I met up again with Dr. Ian Hussein, the cemetery director to find out if I had raised enough for work to start on assembling the memorial, and also if enough support from the different sections of the community had been gained to satisfy the various heritage committees. I received a brief letter from him saying they now had enough support, not only from bereaved parents but also from the general public, and in light of this and coupled with the monies raised, the memorial would be erected, hopefully by 2009.

The chosen angel was removed from its original position and was taken to the workshops, which was in itself a difficult task because of the age and the fragility of the stone.

The Conservation Team cleaned the angel with their specialised cleaning equipment, which is called the JOS/TORC system. This system uses calcium carbonate, approved by English Heritage. The angel was put in position on the marble plinth, the inscription completed and the work began on the pathways leading to the memorial. The cement foundation base was covered with marble and a small 'rockery type' garden surrounds the memorial.

We had many meetings with the Heritage committee, conservation officers, the director of the cemetery Ian Hussein, plus many visits to the cemetery over the years it took before the angel memorial was finally finished and in position. After six long years, we had a date for the unveiling of the angel memorial. It was on Sunday 26th April 2009 at 1pm. The Memorial is for all children whatever their age. The dedication and unveiling ceremony of the memorial angel went perfectly, the sun shone all day; lots of friends, many from TCF attended and it was indeed a very emotional and memorable day - for us and all the bereaved parents who attended.

The service was beautiful, conducted by the Reverend Peter Smith, the vicar of Aldersbrook and assistant area Dean of Redbridge. After the welcome, Mr. Phillip Everett, director of environmental services for the City of London Corporation, gave a short talk about policy of adapting to the needs of the community, of which the memorial angel is an example.

My husband Mike then spoke of the needs of bereaved parents, of how in today's world the anguish of parents bereft of a child is perhaps, less well understood than in times past, and how, generally speaking, the only people who can understand are others who have suffered the same sorrow.

The sense of isolation that arises from the perceived lack of understanding contributes to the suffering. The Compassionate Friends' organisation bridges the gap, enabling bereaved parents to contact one another in order to share in their grief and sorrow and provide mutual, truly understanding support. Mike thanked all those whose efforts had enabled completion of the memorial angel - the City of London Corporation, director Dr. Ian Hussein and his staff, the Rev. Peter Smith, fundraisers from TCF and other friends and family; and to me for providing the inspiration for the memorial.

Finally, we had the unveiling and laying of floral tributes, many from bereaved parents, followed by a deeply appreciated homily given by the Reverend Peter Smith, a message of love and hope, before dedicating and blessing the memorial.

After the ceremony, we all moved to a marquee in the cemetery grounds, where refreshments were served. This was all paid for by the corporation of London for which we were very grateful. As parents sat in the sunshine and chatted and spoke of their beloved children, they left their thoughts of the day in a Remembrance book that was donated by a lovely stationery company, for visitors to the angel memorial and baby garden. This memorial angel is a monument in memory of all our precious children we have tragically lost. It is for all ages and all religions and all belies.

As we all know, losing a child, of whatever age, is the most devastating disaster that can ever happen in a person's lifetime. You never 'come to terms with it' and you never get over it; the grief and pain lives with you forever. This will be a lasting tribute to all our precious children. I myself found that, especially in those dark early days, having this project to focus on, although very daunting, really helped me by focusing my grief into creating a beautiful lasting memorial that would also benefit and help other bereaved parents as well as our own family.

The angel memorial is still visited regularly by groups of bereaved parents, from all over the UK, and even from as far away as America and Australia. We meet many of them at the station, especially if they do not know the area and we escort them the rest of the way to the cemetery."

The Memorial Angel in situ

Through my posts on TCF about the nature of James' death, I was pointed in the direction of the US-based group the Drowning Support Network, which became a great online forum resource for me as well as introducing me to my dear friend Karen.

Nancy Rigg, is the founder of Internet-based groups, the Drowning Support Network and DSN Advocacy. Nancy lost her fiancé, Earl Higgins, in 1980, when he was swept down the flood-swollen Los Angeles river, as he rescued a young boy. She says of that time, "Trauma lingers, and I was compelled to create change in the way flood and swift water rescues are prepared for, responded to, and prevented to begin with."

I strongly believe that Nancy's determination to effect change, which remains undimmed with time, helped her live through her grief for Earl and I have used as a role model her positive attitude to grief – and life in general – ever since I first found DSN on the Internet.

Nancy is wholly committed to her cause; she is a warm and eloquent writer who admirably sustains and supports those who are living through loss.

She says, "For me, the fact that through the Internet, I was able to offer a supportive platform, with reliable information and resources, for bereaved families dealing with sudden death grief and trauma, was important, because when I went through the bewildering and agonising experience in 1980, there was nothing out there – no information on post-traumatic stress, no information on sudden death grief, nothing.

Mine was a lonely and, at times, very agonising experience to go through. I had no family living in this huge metropolis of Los Angeles. Earl and I had only lived here six weeks before he was swept away. And because he was missing for nine months, and there was no-one searching for him, or doing anything to resolve the safety and emergency response issues that compounded his death and prevented his rescue, I did not feel comfortable returning to Colorado where my family lived. So I stayed and started, slowly, to rebuild my life.

Over the years, an entire sub-specialty in mental health has grown around sudden death grief and trauma, so skilled professional help should be available if families are careful in their research and in selecting a specialist to work with.

I was fortunate to work with one of the pioneers in post-traumatic stress research in LA, so I literally helped 'write the book' on the impact of trauma on survivors of natural disasters – in my case, deadly floods. I don't often add the 'D' to PTSD, for 'disorder,' because, as we know now, it is normal rather than unexpected for survivors to be deeply traumatised. If I had had access back then to the information and resources we make available on DSN now, I don't think my own recovery would have been as prolonged as it was, or as complicated. Not that there are any easy fixes! The greatest tool for dealing with the trauma is accurate and reliable information. Education is the key – the education of survivors and the mental health industry."

I think that Nancy really hits the nail on the head when she says that "education is the key", for people remain markedly unaware of the dangers posed by water whether it is the ocean or an inland lake or river and this is even more important in areas of the USA such as California where the climate lends itself to far more leisure activities on water than we are accustomed to in the UK.

I asked Nancy about the origins of DSN and she told me, "Back in the 1990s, an Internet program called eGroups was created and a firefighter friend said, 'Why not set up a support group online?' Hence, the birth of DSN, which was originally designed to serve families dealing with loved ones who were missing in the water, since that is such a difficult challenge for survivors to come to terms with.

Another firefighter friend suggested, 'Why not open the group to all families who have lost someone to drowning or other aquatic tragedy?' And so DSN in its current form came into being.

DSN seems to remain the sole source for the kind of in-depth information we provide on sudden death grief and trauma related to drowning and aquatic tragedies. What makes DSN work as a resource is the common loss that everyone shares."

Nancy explains, "I may have provided the platform and the educational resources, but the members support one another in deeply moving ways. Some people have joined for a little while, receiving needed support and then moving on. But others have joined and then remained members, not just for a year or two, but for several years, lending support to newer members. I never anticipated this 'benefit' when I launched the group. But I believe it has been one of the most important attributes. Those who are several years along in the grief-healing process are not just role models, but they have paved the path for others coming into the group. They are a tremendous resource."

American Mitch Carmody, who lost his son Kelly to cancer in 1987, draws parallels between the first five years of loss and the first five years in a child's life. The start is a blind, ignorant, fumbling, stumbling affair as one struggles to comprehend arriving into a jagged, noisy, discordant world. In his writing, Mitch uses the baby/child model to good effect.

At the time of the child's passing, he says of the parents, "Taken from a world that you knew and understood, a world of warmth and security, you find yourself head first in a cold painful world of the unknown. It's hard to see, you are shaking, insecure and frightened of what's ahead. Tears flow from your eyes, you feel cold and lost and just want someone to hold you and tell you it's just a dream." He asks the reader whether he is describing a baby just being born into this world, or a parent just hearing the news of, or witnessing the death of their child.

He goes on to answer, "It could be both since both describe being thrust into the unknown and faced with the continuing challenges of survival."

But, somehow, survive we do. The first year passes, that crazy time of re-learning how to hold a cohesive thought, how to breathe and move and take baby steps to walk.

At first, the bereaved parent fails to realise how widespread is the ripple effect of their loss. Mitch points out that parents who lose a child have to deal with their own personal grief, the grief of their spouse, their combined grief as parents, the grief of their other children, as well as the grief of the grandparents, the extended family, friends and the world in general. Most parents end up giving more support to others than they receive themselves.

It is true to say that after the loss of a child, all our relationships have, to some degree, been irrevocably altered by our loss.

There is a void that can never be filled, and which is felt especially at significant times such as birthdays and Christmas. Holidays and special occasions are particularly difficult to acclimatise to without that special individual's input. It is very hard to feel celebratory without concomitant guilt at enjoying occasions without the presence of those who are missing.

Mitch also makes a valid point when he says, "When you experience the loss of a significant loved one, you not only lose their presence in your life, you lose all the people and potentials that would have come into your life because of who they were."

This is a concept that is difficult to understand at first but as time passes and we have family weddings and the arrival of grandchildren it is hard not to feel a wistful sadness at the fact that we will never see James marry or have children, and we will never meet colleagues and friends of his. The date that he died is an emphatic full stop and that is very difficult to assimilate.

Mitch talks of a "grief child" which he describes as a "product of your grief" – a result of the transformation of the energy from active grieving. He encourages us to nurture our grief child by accepting the initial despair and pain as being a normal part of the process that will eventually lead to the emergence of a new creature from its cocoon. But this does not happen on its own and it takes a lot of hard work to climb out of the pit of despair and self-pity and rejoin the human race.

Mitch says, "We have suffered, now we must find the gift encapsulated in the grief and find the meaning and purpose this loss has for our life and the lives of others."

He reminds us, "Your loved one can live on through your heart and your hands and your words and still effect change in this world. Love never dies; we have to learn to accept our new relationship; that our child now lives in our heart forever. Living in our heart, our heart has to grow to accommodate their presence in it. Find your own grief child, nurture it and you nurture the world. We substantiate our lost loved one's life by the way we live ours. Let their legacy live on through us and they will live forever. This not only keeps our loved one alive, it heals our heart. Like dropping a pebble into a pond, ripples of love are sent out into the world ad infinitum."

Substantiating the life of someone who has passed too young is difficult for it is almost impossible not to ask the questions, "What would he/she be doing now? Where would they be living? Would they have a partner and children?" As time goes on it is true to say that James' presence feels less substantial that it did when the loss was raw and new. It is only by continually remembering him and referring back to him that I can hold the essence of him. We never forget – how can we? But it is equally very difficult to recall specifics, especially from his earlier years. It is like a gift when someone tells me something they remember of him, or sends me a photo that I haven't seen before. Naturally as time passes, these events lessen, but they are an important aspect of holding the grief close in a positive and helpful way.

Looking again at the bigger picture, rather than just my own loss, I asked my dear friend Karen in Australia, who lost her son Sam to the ocean how she felt at the five-year mark and how she viewed that particular milestone. She replied:

"The five year thing got me musing about how far the world has travelled in that time. It is where his friends are up to in their lives, how grown-up they seem and of course, inevitably, the growing-up that he didn't get to do. Also, technology! Mobile phone ads and the new iPad all make me so sad for what he missed out on. There is so much that I know he would have loved and embraced and I feel so angry about his future just not happening."

I agree with her sentiments of anger entirely and it would be unrealistic not to feel angry at the injustice of untimely bereavement. But we have also discussed the opinion of other people is that our sons' passing is 'such a waste'. The way we view it is that their time here with us was not wasted, not a second of it! Yet what *is* wasted is their opportunity to have a future. I do not think this really resonates until further along the grief path and Karen expresses this evolving emotion very well when she voices her view:

"We are so consumed in those early years by the actual death and loss and horror of it all that it is not until the dust settles a little, so to speak, that we are more aware of what it actually means in terms of the lives they won't get to live and things that they have missed out on. I don't think early on, that we have room in our heads to actually take all that in and it is later - like now and for the future - that we are really hit with it."

It is clear from the foregoing accounts that grief inspires the individual in a variety of ways that help them to confront and deal with their adversity. The words of Sandy, Kelly, Lin, Shaun, Jan, Angela, Nancy, Mitch and Karen, admirably reflect the drive and positivity that can be found despite the tragedy of loss.

Birthday Poem

It is just another day,
But it's the date that you were born,
So perhaps you will indulge us,
In our moments of loss forlorn.

It is just another day, though,
To recall our memories fond,
And to know you are watching over us,
From a better world beyond

It is just another day,
To accept you are in another place,
Not to yearn for that we cannot have,
But to allow the truth with grace

It is just another day,
To mark achievements, great and small,
Progress made in your memory's honour,
So that you are proud of us all

Suddenly, it is just another year,
We've crossed more months without you,
The love remains, the memories too,
To sustain and see us the next year through.

Andrea Corrie, 2009

Chapter 12

Living Today

Maybe

Maybe you were just travelling through
You were not destined to be with us for long
You didn't need to stay a hundred years
To get everything done; you did it in nineteen.
You came to deliver the warmth of your smile
Your lessons in love, friendship and trust
You were already a teacher to us all
To the family and others, so loved ...
Maybe you lived your life faster than the rest
You certainly knew how to make the best
Of all your opportunities, and time;
You wasted nothing, each moment precious.
You delivered your gifts and now you are free
To travel on; an extraordinary being
Who leaves knowledge for we who remain
Your presence to treasure, again and again.

Andrea Corrie, 2007

To conclude this story is difficult because the story of
James, indeed the story of any child's life, does not
conclude. Maybe his was "just another life" spanning
nineteen years before it was cruelly cut short...but the
legacy he left is many things, not just this story.   It is my
story, it is James' story and it is the story of every bereaved
parent.

We all have our own tales to tell, of love for our children and how greatly we miss them after they have gone, each second of every day.

I hope to have provided something of the essence of the vibrant young man who was James. He was a bright, sparky, individual boy, who became a compassionate and caring young man. He would have been a brilliant teacher. He was warm and generous in nature, and he never shied away from showing love and affection to those about whom he cared.

After he learned of James' death, his nephew Ben, who was aged nine at the time, said of him,
"He brought joy," which is a wonderful epitaph.

More recently, I have learned that it is a mistake to think that friends and family do not hold James so much in mind because they mention him less these days.

We had been out to celebrate my birthday and the following morning my sister-in-law Sally emailed to me:
"Last night when I left your house after the lovely evening, I looked up and saw that photo of James, the one in the corner that you took when he was in Brighton, it must have stayed with me as I had a dream of him last night. It was so vivid and I was seeing the dream as if I was saying it like a poem. I woke up and wrote it down while I remembered:

'I saw James
He was walking along through a crowd of people
in the village

I saw James
He was facing away from me, I saw his back
and he was disappearing, like a ship over the horizon

I saw James
I run to follow him, I am closer now
and see the soft curls of hair on his neck

I saw James
I reach out and touch his shoulder, he turns;
the boy has gone, and James is now a man

I saw James
The smile on his lips reaches his eyes,
his whole face is alight with happiness

I saw James
He says 'I am on the way home,
Tell them I am ok'

I saw James."

The comfort provided by such a message is immense, not
least because it emphasises that though James is gone, he is
not by any means forgotten.

James' friend Amy willingly shared her thoughts on how
she feels eight years after James died. She says, "I met
James during my first year at college in Egham, Surrey.
We clicked immediately and soon we were spending all our
free time during college breaks together amongst a group of
close friends. He was such a wonderful friend and
everyone that met him loved him. He was so much fun and
also caring, sensitive and considerate.

My sister and mum, who were used to seeing friends coming and going at home would always take time to ask me, 'How's James?' followed by, 'He's such a lovely guy.'

And he really, truly was. He was also unforgettable – as soon as someone met him, they remembered him. He was a whirlwind of energy and positivity. I can still hear his laugh as clearly as ever today. He had the most wonderful laugh – a proper deep-rooted, hearty laugh that made everyone who heard it smile.

Today, there is not a day that goes by when I do not think of James and say hello in some way. It might be something I see and find funny and know I would have shared with James; and it hurts. It is also those big, life-defining moments – graduation, starting a new job, friends getting engaged or married. It is at those times when the grief physically hurts – like it did at the beginning - and I have to take a step back, reflect and think about what James would want me to do in those moments. I think, for me, when dealing with the grief of losing James, I always think about what James would want me to do.

I do believe that James is still around – his aura, his spirit. He was so full of life and energy and such a wonderful friend that I can't help but still feel that. Although he is not physically here with me, he can still be my best friend - our friendship hasn't, and won't ever, end."

I am grateful for all forms of recognition that James' life did not pass unmarked; my friend Stella, who lives in the US, wrote to me just after the eighth anniversary of James' death, "John and I noted the date this weekend, and found it hard to believe that eight years had elapsed.

I have a school photo of James in a key ring that you gave to me. I use it every day, so he is often in my thoughts.

I know that James would be proud of you and all that you have accomplished in his name. Through you he touches people's lives every day as they walk safely next to the river, and that is a legacy that ensures that he will never be forgotten."

Stella's words about the riverside are underlined by Gary and Tim at Kingston Council. Gary said, "It was only recently that I realised just how much has been achieved and just how substantial an impact has been made on river safety in Kingston. Despite the circumstances you must be very proud at what you achieved in memory of James and I can assure you that as a result many other young lives have been saved; we have evidence to back this claim."

Further, Tim added, "You brought back the memory of those times and, in particular for me, it reminded me of why I worked in local government for so many years which was, in essence, to make a difference for communities by working at a human level with individuals. You were, and remain, an exceptional individual and I am humbled by what you contribute to the benefit of others - your book is further testimony to this."

I have never considered myself to be exceptional. Rather, I think I am an ordinary person to   whom an extraordinary event happened. My reactive response to it was to challenge it, to work with it, and ultimately to force my way through it and come through the other side with the retention of some semblance of sanity.

What more could I want as a legacy for my son than to know his story lives on at Kingston riverside for all time?

It is little compensation for the loss of my bright, articulate, handsome, and above all loving boy, but it is a consolation.

I feel lucky to have the ability to write so that I can cathartically express the emotions surrounding my loss. The written word has the power to release emotions for both writer and reader, which is ultimately helpful.

I like to feel that through my writing, I am helping others to see how they can process their own grief. I like the visualisation of myself as a kind of phoenix rising from the ashes of my grief. It gives me a sense of satisfaction now to share the journey I have taken. The distance from the A to B of grief is long and tortuous, but I have traversed it to arrive at a destination of near contentment, which I could never have anticipated at the start.

Someone asked me recently if it is possible for a bereaved parent ever to be truly happy again. My answer is that pure unadulterated happiness is something that eludes most of us, bereaved or not. But I do believe that it is possible to live with optimism, joy and anticipation again despite knowing the true awfulness of loss. Certainly, I have a much greater appreciation of the transience of life since James died and I do not want to waste the time that I have left, trapped in a place of negativity.

It is the modern way to say that we "own" nebulous things, and I say that we each own our grief. Your sorrow becomes yours and yours alone; how you deal with it becomes a life choice that only you have the ability to make. No-one can influence you about the way you traverse your grief path, but there are many signposts along the way for those who notice them, and who are open to help.

Today, I have learned the lesson that there is no end point to grieving; and the work goes on. I was recently invited to co-present a one-day workshop for bereaved parents. This is a new venture and as such it is a nerve-wracking prospect but if it proves helpful, we shall repeat it. We are a team of four, each of whom has lost a child in entirely different circumstances. So far, we have only met collectively once although there are connections between all of us through our loss and grief paths.

When we met to discuss our programme, I could not help but feel impressed. We represent an amazing testament to the strength of women in general; and mothers in particular. From the depths of the pit of despair in which we all found ourselves early in loss, we have arrived at a place where we are able to reach out and disseminate our grief knowledge to those who are now in greater need. This demonstrates altruism in the real sense of the word; an unselfish concern for the welfare of others. We all have different strengths and our progress in grieving, if it can be thus described, justly honours the memory and the lives of our dear children.

I hope that my story raises the expectations for the future of those who are newly bereaved and broadens the understanding of the grief path in those around them. I am no expert in grief, other than being someone who has lived, and continues to live, through the process.

I offer you my thoughts and I trust that sharing my own experience and touching on the experiences of others, will underline that although we may think so, certainly at first, we are not alone.

Just Visiting

I saw you today! ...
Just a corner of the eye glimpse
As I drove through the town.
You were walking along the pavement
Laughing with your friends
Carefree, handsome, happy
Arms laden with Christmas shopping
Your eyes bright, cheeks flushed
(you'd probably all been to the pub)
I think that if you'd caught sight of me
As I drove slowly past
You would have ignored me
(bad street cred to wave to your mum)
But when I caught up with you at home later
You would have given me a hug
And said,
"Hey mum, was it you I saw ...?"
And although I realised afterwards
It could not possibly be you whom I glimpsed
I held your smile in my thoughts all day
Grateful just to have viewed you in my mind.

Andrea Corrie, 2006

James and I in Brighton, October 2004

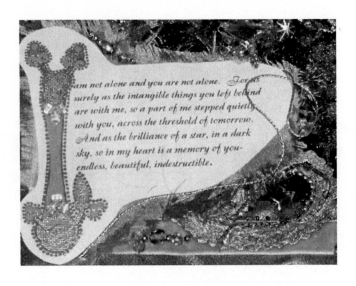

am not alone and you are not alone. For
surely as the intangible things you left behind
are with me, so a part of me stepped quietly
with you, across the threshold of tomorrow.
And as the brilliance of a star, in a dark
sky, so in my heart is a memory of you—
endless, beautiful, indestructible.

Dear James,

Your physical presence is gone, but I can conjure up your
face, your smile, sometimes your voice, in my mind. I see
you in other young men, maybe out running, or working in
the supermarket, perhaps a glimpse when I drive through
town. The likeness to you can make me gasp, whether it is
in the set of a young man's shoulders, his walk or a facial
expression. At first, these incidents would leave me feeling
empty and dissatisfied, but now I take comfort from them.

I know you are not alone. Your father and your
grandparents are with you in spirit. It matters not whether I
or anyone else believes in the afterlife, which does not
affect the truth of your being together. But I believe your
soul lives outside this earthbound plane, and I believe that
you send me signs, such as the dreams when I hear you
telling me, "It's all right, mum, don't worry about me,"
and of course you send us butterflies so regularly as to be
beyond coincidence.

You left behind a wonderful storehouse of memories –
memories that do not and will not fade. You left behind the
impression you made on so many people. You left behind
that remarkable ability to make people happy with your
cheerful presence. You always showed compassion to
those less fortunate and you would have made a brilliant
teacher. Of course, you were no angel; you were the boy
who sat on the settee all day on a Sunday watching
television. But the greatest intangible thing you bequeathed
me is pride; the pride that I felt from the moment you were
born, to that dreadful moment when we knew you were lost
to us and beyond.

The part of me that gave you life, that nurtured you in the
womb, which contributed to your physical being, your very
DNA that you are, stepped quietly with you that day. But
you left behind the light that illuminated your soul. I know
James, that you shine on in the darkness of our grief.

Dearest son, I love you always,

Mum xxx

Useful Information

The list that follows is intended to be a useful reference guide and is populated via the contributors to the book. I bear no responsibility for the accuracy, content or legality of any linked site or organisation that is listed here, or for that of any subsequent links. The web addresses are accurate at the time of going to press.

Some have associated Facebook pages and/or groups or may be found using Google search or similar.

Also, I shall not be liable for any losses or damages (including without limitation consequential loss or damage) whatsoever from the use of, or reliance on, the advice provided. Any links to other Web sites or organisations does not constitute an endorsement or an approval by myself of any products, services, policies or opinions of the organisation or individual. The list is in no particular order of preference.

The Compassionate Friends (UK and United States)
http://www.tcf.org.uk/
http://www.compassionatefriends.org/home.aspx

Drowning Support Network USA
http://health.groups.yahoo.com/group/DrowningSupportNetwork/
http://groups.yahoo.com/group/DSNAdvocacy/

CRUSE Bereavement Services UK
http://www.cruse.org.uk

Jan Andersen (author of Chasing Death: Losing a Child to Suicide)
http://www.childsuicide.org

Harry Edwards Healing Sanctuary UK
http://www.harryedwardshealingsanctuary.org.uk/

Mitch Carmody USA
http://heartlightstudios.net/

Celia Marchisio (Reiki)
http://www.spiritualvoice.co.uk/

Chalice Well, Glastonbury
http://www.chalicewell.org.uk/

Sandra Totterdell (art)
http://www.outsidein.org.uk/sandra-totterdell

Carmella B'Hahn
Books available from Carmella's website
http://www.SolaceAlchemy.com
'Benjaya's Gifts'
'Mourning has Broken: Learning from the Wisdom
Of Adversity'

Lisa De Souza Portraits and Keepsakes
https://www.facebook.com/LisaDeSouza.PortraitsandKeeps
akes

Proofreader
Ann Hopkins
ann.hopkins@talk21.com

9 781905 399895